S0-EDH-753

THE
TWENTY-FIVE CENT
GAMBLE

THE
TWENTY-FIVE CENT
GAMBLE

June Duran Stock

authorHOUSE®

AuthorHouse™
1663 Liberty Drive
Bloomington, IN 47403
www.authorhouse.com
Phone: 1-800-839-8640

© 2013 by June Duran Stock. All rights reserved.

No part of this book may be reproduced, stored in a retrieval system, or transmitted by any means without the written permission of the author.

Published by AuthorHouse   11/15/2012

ISBN: 978-1-4772-8758-3 (sc)
ISBN: 978-1-4772-8757-6 (hc)
ISBN: 978-1-4772-8756-9 (e)

Library of Congress Control Number: 2012920836

This book is printed on acid-free paper.

Because of the dynamic nature of the Internet, any web addresses or links contained in this book may have changed since publication and may no longer be valid. The views expressed in this work are solely those of the author and do not necessarily reflect the views of the publisher, and the publisher hereby disclaims any responsibility for them.

CONTENTS

ACKNOWLEDGEMENTS

This book would not have been possible without the help and encouragement of so many:

Ellen Haley, whose interest in CTB's history kept me in focus; Laura and Brian Dadiw, whose unfailing guidance and assistance has been so important; George Gracey, New Cumberland (Pennsylvania) branch manager, who's been through it all; John Stewart, one of the original band of CTB consultants, who helped reminisce about the old days; Paul Lee, for his friendship and guidance during the sale and transfer of CTB to McGraw-Hill in 1965; Doug Hartman and Larry Acquistapace, for so much help locating and sharing CTB archives; Bob Stock, for his exceptional photographic and deciphering capabilities; Harvey Sullivan along with Tonni Larsen, Roger Creamer, Bill Satchell, and Joanne Millard for their important input on data processing and reporting; Ron Weitzman, whose strong background in educational statistics greatly influenced the inclusion of the Appendix; David Taggart and Meredith Mullins, who helped me see the value of writing the book; Adele Brandstrom, for her exceptional help editing the manuscript; Kit Artig, for her creative talent; and my husband, Morgan Stock, for his patient endurance.

I'm sure I've omitted the names of many others who contributed, some just by a chance remark, a memory, or the work they shared with me. To all those: my deep gratitude and appreciation along with my apologies.

June Duran Stock
2012

PREFACE

It was my mother who took the gamble.

It was a gamble that paid off quite handsomely from her investment of a grand total of twenty-five cents. Women were not active in business in 1926. They did not start their own companies, and they certainly did not make a foray into the business world without telling their husbands what they were doing.

However, that is exactly what my mother, Ethel M. Clark, did. Perhaps keeping her venture from her husband, Willis W. Clark, was the foreshadowing of what developed into a world of guile and sometimes sleight of hand to maneuver her little kitchen company into a leading publisher of educational tests for students ranging from kindergarten to high school.

When she made her investment of twenty-five penny postcards, she had no business experience, no business plan, no strategy, no long-term goals, and no idea of market penetration. Her venture did not even have a name or an address except for a private residential address. All she had was the determined hope that the investment would help her "be somebody."

This, then, is the true story of two remarkable people who—through luck, conflict, determination, and perseverance—saw the growth of an idea that was spawned from my mother's imagination to provide positive value to the country's educational system. The struggles, precarious relationships, financial difficulties, and incredible foresight were the basis of many formidable scenes. Yet there were moments of understanding and compassion, which are treasures among all my memories of my parents. Maybe, at times, the story will appear judgmental, but it was set down with great love and sincere admiration.

Ethel, with her compelling, dynamic, and, at times, outrageous personality, and Willis, with his mild, studious, and philosophical demeanor, made a most unlikely team. They are, without any doubt, the stars of the story. There is also a supporting cast, including Warren, Frank, and me—and that insidious scar, which played such a diabolical role in our relationships. The results are irrefutable, and so here it is laid out for you: "The Twenty-Five Cent Gamble."

CHAPTER 1

AN UNEQUAL PARTNERSHIP

My name is June. I am Willis and Ethel Clark's only child. I am the sole survivor of those turbulent years, so, by default, I become the narrator of the memories and stories of how my mother's gamble paid off—how she mastered the illusory nature of life and business and molded those illusions to suit her needs, achieve her goals, and create a world that shaped her life and the lives of everyone around her. I am also the cause of the scar. My mother was a beautiful woman, the type of woman who knew everything about her body—every mole, blemish, vein, and wrinkle. The scar was something visible, tangible, touchable; corporeal evidence she could always hold up to me as an excuse for her lifelong attempt to keep me at a distance and to remind both of us of what, in her mind, was the beauty that was so violently ripped from her.

It would be easier to tell two stories, one about my mother and the other about the company, but the two are so inexorably intertwined that they cannot be separated. She would have been an interesting character without starting an important business. It was her nature to star in her own life regardless of its circumstances. She would never let anyone else define her or categorize her. Her relationship with my father was very strange by other families' standards, but the two of them developed an unspoken allegiance.

I decided to share their unique story and the growth and development of their company. Yes, their company, for despite Ethel's colorful and outspoken demeanor, it was Willis's work that in the long run became the heart of "CTB," the California Test Bureau.

But first, I needed to refresh my memory, so in 2008 I decided to visit what is now CTB/McGraw-Hill.

*   *   *

The Monterey Peninsula is the crown jewel in the necklace of cliffs and coves that line the entire length of the California coast, from its northern boundary with Oregon down to the Mexican border. The breathtaking view of the city of Monterey with its spectacular harbor lay before me as I approached the CTB/McGraw-Hill building. The serenity of the coastline was in direct contrast to the apprehension that overtook me when I reached that gargantuan fortress of a building. Immediately questions and doubts flooded my mind as to whether or not I would be able to tell the story of all that had happened. I wondered why I was doing this, and whether this trip was only a fantasy.

I didn't know what I would learn about my parents when I walked through that door at CTB/McGraw-Hill. So many memories flooded my mind. Some were memories that a child should not have about her mother—memories that any child would be hesitant to include in a story about her parents—because they are so different than memories most children have . . .

Imagine it being Christmastime and being no more than four years old. A terrible argument is raging in the house. It awakens you and, as you slip the misty bond of sleep, you realize the shouting is coming from the voices of your mother and father. You get out of bed. Your feet reluctantly lead you to the shouting voices. Slowly you walk into the little den where the noise is coming from. With wide-eyed disbelief you see your mother pointing a gun at your father. Your father is trying to calm her down. You are a child, but you know what a gun can do. They suddenly see you. It is a surreal moment, almost inexplicable. Seconds go by, but it seems like hours, as your parents look to one another, then at you. You can see panic in your father's blue-grey eyes. Ethel is calm as she casually puts the gun down. And that is the end of it. You have no idea what transpired to cause such a situation. You are not even sure you remember it correctly. It was all so long ago. But you do remember getting up on Christmas morning to find a little dog named Homer tied to the Christmas tree in the den—the same den where the gun was.

 . . . The memory slowly faded away. Even though I reined in my emotions, my own resolve almost melted. I started to turn around to go home when a friendly voice called out, "Hello June," and there was no going back. I was guided to the reception desk to sign in and receive the badge that would transport me through my journey back to the past. I took a moment to revisit Willis Clark's memorial oak cabinet, now a permanent fixture at CTB. My father's most treasured text references and a copy of his first major test, the *Progressive Achievement Test,* were visible through the glass panels. It was a bittersweet moment as I saw the pictures of both my parents, Ethel and Willis Clark, on top of the cabinet. My mother was the founder, and Willis, her partner, developed the tests for CTB. At least outwardly they were partners, but I came to realize, as I became more mature and discerning, the partnership was not an equal one.

CHAPTER 2

THE BIG PICTURE

There are times, even from my point of view as their only child, when it seems so incomprehensible two diverse personalities such as Ethel and Willis could ever get together. Willis was a serious, studious, quietly ambitious young man focused on new educational theories and their positive impact on the futures of individual students. Ethel was a beautiful, dynamic, aspiring young woman with a strong personality and a resemblance to Joan Crawford—one of the most recognizable movie stars of the day. That is not to say Ethel would have thought of herself as Joan Crawford. If anything, she would have felt comfortable with others comparing Crawford to her. Besides, Crawford was definable by the roles she played on the screen. Ethel was her own woman and would remain so all of her life. Perhaps what defined Joan Crawford were the roles she played as the prototypical indomitable woman succeeding in a man's world—in that respect the screen persona of Crawford and the real persona of Ethel Clark were comparable. There is no doubt in my mind, as Ethel's child, that going head-to-head with Ethel, Crawford would be relegated to the back lot.

My mother always saw the big picture. My father was more involved in the minutiae of the nuts and bolts part of the business, which was a very important aspect of what they did, but Ethel could always see what was coming around the bend. Her big-picture outlook served the family well when my parents moved the company to Monterey on the Central California Coast. Ethel said there was only so much land in the world that sat on an ocean's shore, and she wanted some of it. When she saw the lot in Pebble Beach, she envisioned the views she would see from her windows. She had the foresight to purchase five lots rather than only one for the homestead.

Ethel painted in broad strokes while my father focused on and filled in the details with a fine brush. I think her ability to have such a panoramic view of the business they were creating was most responsible for her not having doubts or misgivings about whatever project she undertook. So many of her decisions were made correctly and were made without the benefit of consultation—or, for that matter, without the benefit of research—that it was almost as if she had prescient knowledge of how things would turn out.

* * *

Willis Winfield Clark was born in Ancona, Illinois, March 26, 1895, and was raised on a farm in a small town in South Dakota. That doesn't mean there were limitations to his formal education. The farm did present him with endless opportunities to keep his inquisitive mind active and busy. His father decided to move from the huge farmlands he owned in South Dakota to see whether he would like the city life of Los Angeles, where there were so many more opportunities, especially educational opportunities. Yet he knew that everyone would not like the move, so he gave his four children the option to either take one fourth of the farmland or get a college education in Southern California. Willis and his sister Marie opted for the college education while their two siblings chose to split the farmlands that even today remain in family hands.

My mother was born Ethel May King in 1901 in Madison, Indiana. Ed and Jen King had desperately wanted a boy, so when Ethel was born, they went as far as dressing her as a boy. She became the center of their universe, but her status in the family was quickly reduced when Richard was born. He was seven years younger and always seemed to have the upper hand with his parents' affections. No longer was Ethel's hair put in curls for special occasions, nor was she allowed new shoes for Easter. Richard was the one who could always wheedle a few pennies from his mother from her meager, well-hidden budget money—but there was none for Ethel. It is easy to speculate that she may have worn slacks as an adult far in advance of most women in Los Angeles because her parents insisted on trying to make her into a boy. The favoritism for Richard grew until it became a lifetime rivalry between the two siblings. Ethel paid for her own education, yet when it was time for Richard's schooling, her parents paid for his.

When Ethel's father was offered a job, the King family made their way from Indiana to California, settling in the Los Angeles area. Willis's sister Marie and Ethel met when they both enrolled at Manual Arts High School. School was a wonderful escape for Ethel from her overindulged younger brother. The school was founded in 1910 at 4131 South Vermont Avenue and is the oldest high school still on its original site in the Los Angeles Unified School District. The name of the school embodied the principles of head, heart, and hand, offering a creative atmosphere for the full life. Cartoonist Gus Arriola, who lived in Carmel (south of Monterey) for much of his life, is among the famous persons who went to Manual Arts. Film director Frank Capra, actress Kathryn Grayson, actor Paul Winfield, World War II ace Jimmy Doolittle, and author Irving Stone are among the school's other renowned graduates. Artist Jackson Pollack, who would have been in the class of 1930, left before graduation.

Ethel and Marie became good friends. Although they came from different backgrounds, they had much in common and shared many of the same dreams and goals. Marie, like Ethel, wanted to break out from the shadow of a brother and be her own person. Willis, who was that older brother, was at the University of Southern California (USC) working on his bachelor's degree. As studious as he was, he managed to find time to be very kind and attentive to Marie and her friend Ethel. Willis may have immersed himself in his studies, but he was attracted by Ethel's beauty. If her good looks caught his eye, her fiery determination was even more of an attraction. He may have seen his alter ego in her. She must have been quite a departure from the girls he knew in South Dakota, and the fact that she was a friend of his sister also may have been an important factor in his getting to know her. She was there. No searching was necessary. He didn't have to take time away from his studies to seek female companionship on the crowded USC campus.

Ethel and Marie graduated from high school in June 1916, and Willis received a B.A. from USC the same year. He spent the following year at Columbia University in the New York School of Social Work. Then it was back to USC for an M.A. he received in 1918. While splitting his time between the two coasts, he never lost contact with

Ethel. He kept in constant contact with her, carrying on a courtship that was far from traversing constellations across a summer sky but may have had enough of the elements of an astrophysical romance to win her over.

Willis was attracted to Ethel for many reasons. She had absolutely gorgeous, big brown eyes that highlighted her olive complexion. She had beautiful hair that she braided as a teenager and then wore in coils around her ears, in the style of the day. They both liked hiking, something they did often. It was time shared together and an activity that didn't cost any money. Ethel joked that she was straight up and down—like a boy—when they met, but Willis described her as being lithe and athletic. She was tall at 5'6", just a couple of inches shorter than Willis.

Ethel was certainly attracted to his blue-grey eyes, a perfect complement to his fair complexion. He had a full head of sandy hair (which turned gray at an early age). He, too, was athletic. In college he participated in gymnastics and was particularly good at the pommel horse.

The two were married March 16, 1918, in a simple church wedding with the only witnesses the pastor, his wife, and daughter. The wedding was quiet, informal, and was not attended by any other family members, which may have been a result of the financial situation of the day. Ethel's father kept a daily record of every penny spent in a beat-up, old black ledger. The thought of parting with any sum to finance his daughter's wedding may have burst the binding on the old ledger. Sometimes though, my mother could resort to darker harmonies and be quite devious. She admired Willis as a person of substance and vision. She simply may have wanted to spirit him away before any other woman could recognize the fine qualities she saw in him. Still, it was a tranquil beginning to a turbulent future, made all the more turbulent by the United States declaring war on Germany in April 1917 and Congress passing the Selective Service Act in May 1917.

CHAPTER 3

BEING SOMEBODY

Ethel was determined to "be somebody." She knew this could not happen within the family structure, so she borrowed money to enroll in secretarial school. Ethel understood that any advancement to her career must come through education and acquiring skills that were useful in the business world. She recognized the value of attaining secretarial skills as the industrial expansion that had been going on since the turn of the century caused a paperwork crisis in offices. Secretaries adapted to new technologies such as the adding and calculating machine, telephone, and typewriter. As the demand for secretaries increased, women rushed in to fill the need. Secretarial jobs provided the chance for women to break away from domestic jobs and positions as sales clerks. They could work outside the home in a business atmosphere that was previously closed to them. They attended secretarial schools and worked to attain superior skills. The demand for secretaries was so great that it outpaced the supply. Ethel was among the many women vying for positions as secretaries. Ethel's determination turned her into a proficient typist. She used her skill to support herself by typing theses and dissertations.

Meanwhile Ethel's brother Richard exhibited his own determination at USC, where he majored in architecture. While he was still a student, he won a national architecture contest sponsored by *Pencil Points* magazine, which today is called *Progressive Architecture*. The award included a trip to Europe along with considerable publicity. He was drafted into the Army, for he had been an ROTC enlistee, or at least he served in Monterey at the Presidio as an ROTC officer in the cavalry. During the war, Richard was selected to be Post Engineer at Fort McArthur in San Pedro, California. Richard appeared dashing in a uniform. He had a bit of a swagger and always seemed a little cocky. Richard loved the Army and was proud of his position. He was eventually transferred to Thule, Greenland, as Post Engineer but was released and no details are known.

Ethel got some satisfaction in a perverse way one time when she and Willis rented a cabin in Big Bear Lake, and Richard, Ed, and Jen came for a visit. For some reason Ethel, Willis, and Richard decided to go horseback riding. Ethel was not particularly enthused to get on a horse. Richard had a very high-spirited horse and kept racing back to Ethel, urging her on. Then he would race forward a few hundred yards and then back again in a swirl of dust, showing off with his swashbuckling demeanor for his parents. Ethel's horse became agitated and started to chase Richard's. Ethel was terrified at the speed of her horse. She lost her balance, fell off, and broke her leg. Ed was furious with Richard for teasing Ethel's horse in such a way. It took a broken leg, but, for once, Ethel was the center of attention.

Richard became a well-known architect and did a lot of work for people in the movies. Some years after divorcing his first wife, he met and married a very sweet, pretty young lady named Janice. Richard was a heavy drinker—a surprise considering my grandparents were teetotalers. It was an anomaly that both their children abused alcohol when they became adults. He could turn almost instantly from a charming fellow to a mean drunk if he was challenged in any way. I don't know whether Janice incited the incidents, but I remember angry rows that could escalate into a fight with any man who seemed to be flirting with Janice.

Years later Ethel would have a great deal of repressed satisfaction when Richard became the subject of an infamous headline story in Los Angeles. Richard and Janice built a beautiful home on Bristol Avenue in Brentwood, California. They lived next to a movie star and ran around with that kind of high-stepping crowd. Janice was very mild tempered and was all but cowed by Richard most of the time. She took care of herself, dressing nicely and appearing well coifed and manicured with almost professional looking make-up. However, she had to absolutely beg Richard to get money for a new dress, or even, at times, for food for the household. He was constantly suspicious of her. It turned out that Richard had reason for his feelings, for when he came home unexpectedly one afternoon, he found Janice in bed with her hairdresser. He took military action—he got his gun and shot at her. The shot grazed her hip. Then realizing what he had done, he turned the gun on himself and shot off the side of his face, including an eye.

I was with Ethel, Willis, and Warren, a friend of the family, driving to Las Vegas when this made the news. We first heard it on the car radio with absolute disbelief, but then we realized it had to be *that* Richard King, so we turned around and drove back home while breaking several speed records. My grandfather, Eddie King, a retired Detective Lieutenant on the Los Angeles homicide squad, was thrown into the awkward position of trying to help Richard, even though it was obvious what had happened. Richard spent more than two years going through plastic surgery and hospitalization at Sawtelle Veterans Hospital, where he developed yellow jaundice. My grandfather must have pulled in every marker he had because Richard never did any jail time. I visited him several times at the hospital. It was painful to see what this handsome, intelligent man had done to himself.

He and Janice eventually divorced, and she and their two children had a terrible time adjusting to it all. Janice had begun drinking copious amounts of wine before the accident. I was with her and Richard one evening at a restaurant when she passed out, the very caricature of a drunk with her head on the dinner plate. I had a hard time believing it. I liked Janice despite the tragedy, and she must have sensed it, for she kept calling me from an alcoholic recovery facility. She begged me to get her out. Although I felt sorry for her, there was nothing I could do to get her released. It is impossible to surmise what brought this beautiful and popular couple to such a disastrous state.

Both Ethel and Richard had strong, compelling personalities. Their infrequent meetings throughout their lives crackled with palpable dislike and distrust of each other, each trying to outdo the other in obtaining the favor of their parents. Ethel's contributions and incredible success in the business world would be overlooked as being of no consequence. Although in the long run Richard was the loser, the many years until his untimely death were filled with Ethel's understandable envy and resentment. The only thing they enjoyed in common was their love for dogs. The conversation between them would stay safe as long as that was the subject. Other than that, who had the best house, the best vacation, or had done the most for their mother and father was often the basis for continuing harangues.

Ethel managed to hold her own against her brother, perhaps honing the skills that would serve her so well in the future when she had to make her place in a male-dominated business. Years later I came to believe my mother's desire to escape her second-class status at home may have been the real incentive for her marriage to my father.

Richard died in Needles, California, where he was working in some capacity as an architect. Apparently alcohol was a contributing factor to his death. My grandparents were devastated by everything related to the shooting and the events that transpired afterward. Richard had kept his Colonel's uniform and my grandmother kept bringing it out and sobbing over it for years. My grandfather would try to soothe her, but I know his heart was broken too. They were never the same.

CHAPTER 4

"HELP THE TEACHER
HELP THE CHILD"

There were tough financial times at the beginning of married life for Ethel and Willis. It was wartime and the nation was in turmoil. Patriotism was at paroxysmal heights, with young, fit men of military age lining up to enlist. Willis had a heart murmur so was unable to enlist. He continued his studies at USC and was accepted as a field worker and sociologist by the California Bureau of Juvenile Research for employment at the Whittier State School for Boys (subsequently known as the Fred C. Nelles School for Boys). The work was interesting, but the pay was low. Ethel contributed to their financial stability and remained a major support through her work as a typist for professors at USC.

Of course there were the normal adjustments for a young married couple. Ethel was getting bored with the continual routine of her typing jobs. The preparation of meals and the usual household chores were not the least bit interesting to her. She did enjoy trying out new recipes and occasionally went to demonstration classes, where new ways of preparing food were presented. She even began compiling an extensive file of recipes, a habit that continued for most of her life. She took pride in decorating and redecorating their little bungalow and loved, even then, to give rather outrageous parties.

The Clarks had a piano that Ethel now and then attempted to play. Willis had studied cornet as an elective, but when they tried to play duets, it was readily apparent that they were never going anywhere with their act. Usually they couldn't even agree on what music to play. It was awful. Ethel liked modern, peppy songs and Willis the classics. Believe me, "I Dreamed I Dwelt in Marble Halls" was not a success story. Ethel began to make fun of Willis's efforts on the cornet, and he finally stopped playing. It was typical that those two diverse personalities were unable to agree on many, simple things. Despite that, once in a while they would sing to each other. Victor Herbert's "Gypsy Love Song" and "There's a Long, Long Trail," a war song of that time, were favorites. I loved to hear them, both songs obviously having some special meaning to them.

Willis enjoyed roundelays but not the ones commonly sung such as "Row, Row, Row Your Boat." His were more sophisticated. His favorite was "The Dame's Crane," which went:

> My dame had a lame, tame crane
> My dame had a crane that was lame
> Oh, pray gentle Jane that my
> Dame's lame, tame crane
> Will drink and come home again.

He relished novel ideas, especially those that were new to him, and he loved to try them out. He observed that if one removes the top from a can of dog food, it is still difficult to remove the food. After studying the problem, he reached a solution through trial and error: he cut a hole in the bottom of the can, held it to his mouth, blew hard, and the food came right out. Once he discovered this, he made more applications using the same principle. It worked with all sorts of canned foods. He got a real kick out of doing this.

Many of the problems Willis tackled were so simply solved that I wondered why no one else had solved them sooner. His solution for preventing our dog from pestering him was to spread a thin layer of peanut butter on a pie pan, set it down on the floor, and let the dog spend hours licking it and leaving him alone.

One of Willis's first jobs at the Whittier State School for Boys is described in his own words:

> This was back when I was with the Whittier State
> School doing juvenile research. The state appropriated the
> money to find out how many feeble minded children there

were in Southern California so they could decide how big Pacific Colony should be. (Pacific Colony was an institution for care and housing of what we would today call the developmentally challenged.) I think they could have done it with practically no expense at all by finding out what 3 per cent of the population is, which would have given them a good estimate. But we went out and actually tested students in all the various cities and counties in Southern California. We got actual names and cases so they could make a dollar estimate for Pacific Colony.

During his university studies Willis had become extremely interested in John Dewey's "progressive education" philosophy, which Dewey set forth in his celebrated work *Human Nature and Conduct* (1922). Dewey's concept embodied two elements: (1) the belief that each individual should be recognized for his or her own abilities, interests, ideas, needs, and cultural identity; and (2) the development of critical and socially engaged intelligence, which enables individuals to understand and participate effectively in the affairs of their community in collaborative efforts to achieve a common good. Dewey believed that learning was active and that schooling was unnecessarily long and restrictive. He believed that education should teach children to live in a community and should provide them with real-life experiences so they could contribute to society. He thought that mathematics could be taught by relating it to real experiences, such as determining how long it takes to get from one place to another.

Willis's interest, spurred on by his background and his work at Nelles in the case history method (an extension of Dewey's thinking), involved giving tests individually and recording the scores as part of each boy's personal record. He was never shaken from his belief in the case history philosophy as the way to gain as much knowledge as possible about a student in order to help that person achieve his or her maximum potential. Quantifying that information made it possible for more students to be helped. Articulating and validating the various levels of a given test would make it possible to make more accurate comparisons of individual achievement.

His aim was to calculate an individual's achievement and to record those findings on an easy-to-understand graph, which he called a "profile," whereby a teacher, parent, student, or administrator could see, at a glance, where the individual stood and where the strengths and weaknesses of that person lay. Appropriate remedial work could then be given where it was most needed.

His ultimate goal was to determine a subject's anticipated achievement and derive the formula for that educational application. In his eyes, putting this all together was what educational measurement was all about.

However, to give the test to each individual boy took a great deal of time. There was no way for all of them to be tested. Willis kept thinking about this, wondering whether there was a way to quantify the tests so they could be given in a group. This, in fact, was the genesis of his life's work.

My father concentrated on norm-referenced tests (yielding an estimate of the position of the tested individual in a predefined population, with respect to the trait being measured) despite the fact there were many forms of tests. He set his focus there because those types of tests lent themselves to individual, class, and even school district comparisons to identify primarily the weak spots in the classroom instruction or curriculum. He developed a *Diagnostic Analysis of Learning Difficulties* guide to help with those decisions. This indicated specifically what each item tested and which answers the students marked incorrectly. Each answer was identified to show the particular aspect of the subject matter being tested. The teacher could plot how each student did, the wrong answers could be compiled for study, and remedial work could be undertaken. Willis often used the phrase "Help the teacher help the child."

CHAPTER 5

A BORED CALIFORNIA HOUSEWIFE

Ethel became pregnant late in 1918. The pregnancy carried over to the hot Los Angeles spring when temperatures broke the 100-degree mark, so she suffered through a very difficult period. She could no longer sit at a typewriter, nor perform many of her day-to-day duties. She longed for the birth to happen, so she could be freed from the unbearable confinement. Nothing consoled her, not even Willis's solicitous attempts to be understanding and helpful.

She was taken to Los Angeles General Hospital early in the morning on June 9, 1919, where she went into a lengthy labor. The long labor session sapped her strength until the doctor believed he had no alternative but to perform a Caesarian operation, an uncommon procedure in those days. The next day the doctor operated. He cut a slit in Ethel's beautiful body from just under her breastbone clear down to her pelvic region to assure the baby would not be injured. The baby (me) was delivered in good shape, but Ethel was left with a repulsive, ugly, horrid, jagged scar and a daily reminder of her disfigured body. For years Ethel had a habit of walking around the house naked as if she were intentionally reminding herself of her disfigurement—something she could continually blame on her husband and daughter. I don't think my mother recognized blame as a control mechanism since she was such a controlling person anyway. The scar was simply one more weapon in her arsenal, and the scar was one she could manifestly point to and would use against my father and me for the rest of her life.

The baby confronted the Clarks with a major decision. Willis needed to do something to prevent his future from being tied to a delinquent boys' school, hardly the place for a little girl to be raised. He took a job in 1922 as Assistant Director of Research with the Los

16

Angeles City Schools. There he met Caroline Armstrong, a colleague who shared his interest and enthusiasm for helping teachers identify the weak points in their pupils' scholastic achievement. The common, existing practice required teachers to create their own quizzes to measure student progress, but there was no uniform way to compare one class with another, and the quality of the items on the quizzes varied considerably from teacher to teacher. This method also led to subjective rather than objective comparisons of results, and the schools had no way of knowing how their own classes ranked with others.

Their desire to find a way to alert teachers to individual student weaknesses and to provide comparisons led Willis and Caroline to develop a series of tests called the *Los Angeles Fundamentals of Arithmetic Tests*. These tests broke down the various elements of mathematics into addition, subtraction, division, long division, fractions, etc. Willis described his thoughts this way:

> Well, when you're testing arithmetic, it is something specific. You've got to be able to add, multiply, subtract, or divide. And being able to add requires that you know your combinations and that you are able to do column addition. You should be able to carry if there's any carrying required. When you get down to fractions, you've got to know the meaning of the denominator. Then add the numerators and you have to know how to do a certain number of those things—about ninety things altogether and then you can do arithmetic. So we've had it analyzed as to what these skills are. It doesn't make any difference what textbook you're using; these things are always necessary if you're going to master arithmetic. But in terms of evaluating a given person we do it by our profile method and through our knowledge of learning difficulties—we give a diagnosis of where the person stands. The teacher will know where that person is weak, in what areas, and then will be able to give extra help.

Subsequently the series of tests was expanded to include reading and mechanics of English.

Willis was able to apply his "profiling" method, whereby teachers could mark a student's results on a chart and see, at a glance, in which areas special attention should be given. The fact that the answers were marked right on the test booklet also provided the teacher with insights as to exactly where each individual was going wrong with the arithmetic calculations. These insights helped the teacher help the child. The tests were received with considerable enthusiasm, and a number of other school districts expressed an interest in acquiring copies for their own use.

For her part, Ethel was staying home in their little bungalow with Baby June while all this activity and the incubation of the new testing methods were going on. Her joy over the acceptance the testing was receiving was mitigated by her confinement, and a bit of resentment crept in. Her energy reluctantly was spent on uninteresting and mundane tasks such as cooking and straining vegetables (there was no prepared baby food in jars), washing, dusting, making bread, and other tedious jobs. Ethel was not the kind of woman who wanted to be stuck with housework.

It was at this time her latent interest in style surfaced. Even as they struggled with finances, she managed to look "put together." She went comfortably from the era of hobble skirts and braided hair to the Roaring Twenties era with its flapper styles. She was always in style. She bobbed her hair much to her mother's horror. Only "suspect" ladies were doing that. A single woman cutting her hair short was practically admitting she was no longer a virgin. Women discarded their restrictive girdles and corsets and bound their breasts flat to achieve the masculine look "comme le garçon," like a boy. Soon she was dancing the Charleston. Just as she was eager to break free from restrictive undergarments, she became more eager to break out of her confined life.

She became increasingly restless, and, when she learned from Willis that there was a possibility that the *Fundamentals* series could be published and sold outside the Los Angeles City School District, she began to wonder whether there could be a role for her in this. Her restlessness and fertile imagination led her to explore any role she could play.

In an interview about how she got the idea of starting a test publishing business, Ethel said:

In 1925 my husband was assistant director of research in the Los Angeles City schools. He and several other people had been assigned the task of producing some tests to be used in the Los Angeles City schools. They were made on Los Angeles City time and were printed at Manual Arts High School. Willis kept coming home in the evening and telling me about the various requests for these tests from cities other than Los Angeles. I kept thinking what could be done about this, and I finally made a very grave decision. We at that time had a superintendent by the name of Susan Dorsey in the Los Angeles City schools. You have to be young and very foolish to do things like this, but I wrote her a letter asking for an appointment. I requested of her the right to use the test plates from Manual Arts High School, print the tests on my own, and sell them outside of Los Angeles City. Well, of course, they had to have a board meeting and that took a little time, but finally they consented to my wish. During this time I did not tell my husband anything about what I had done. There was no need to and besides I thought I was really doing something fine that he would appreciate.

I bought 25 postcards and sent them out to 25 different cities that I could remember he had mentioned as wanting to use these tests. Nowadays you can't get a penny postcard, but in those days you could so that was an investment of 25 cents and a long period of agony. The agony came from waiting. I was an impatient person, wanting everything to happen quickly, in my own time.

I didn't think that anything would really come of this matter and I didn't know anything about printing anyway. In fact, looking back, I can't believe I was so bold since I knew very little about any of the testing procedures. A year went by. My grandfather had died, and I came back from the funeral to find in the mailbox an order for 20,000 of one of the tests from Kansas City, Missouri. Needless to say I was on the spot then. I thought the world was coming to an end since I had to tell my husband. He criticized me and told me he would probably lose his job as a result. So I was on my own. I took June in a go-cart and walked down the street to find a printer.

This was in 1926. Van Velzers located on Vermont Avenue in Los Angeles was the first print shop I came to. I showed them the test order. Naturally their first concern was how I was going to pay for the printing. I had no idea how I was going to do that. We already had a mortgage on the house. My husband was fighting me and said I should never have gotten into this type of thing.

We got a second mortgage that paid for the first 20,000 tests. The tests were printed, and they were delivered at our house and put in the garage. Shipping was another part of the procedure I knew nothing about so I simply wrapped the tests and put them in a great big old piano box. I accomplished this with my mother's help. Our inexperience really showed when the bottom then fell out of the box because we put too much weight into it and we had to start all over again. Finally they were shipped and on their way.

When Willis was asked about how he felt when he found out that Ethel had contacted his boss about getting printing plates for his tests, he responded, "I was kind of dubious about what she was getting into and about what my future would be as a result. I didn't have anything much to do with CTB until about 1944, which was about 20 years after she got the thing going, although I always knew what was going on around the Test Bureau."

No orders came in for a long time after the initial order from Kansas City. Dr. Thomas MacQuarrie, who was president of San Jose State College, contacted Ethel about a test of mechanical ability he had developed and asked whether Ethel would publish it. "Of course, I agreed." said Ethel. "With that I realized that I had to get out of a residential area and open an office someplace else which was zoned for business."

The *MacQuarrie Test for Mechanical Ability* was a huge success as a predictor. At a later date it played an important role in the history of the company. Ethel said:

I believe it was in the year 1929 when I was determined to go into the printing business but there were other problems. We sold our house near Normandie Avenue School where June was attending and moved to Alta Vista Boulevard right off of Beverly Boulevard and I rented half of a small building. The printing press was a little Miehle press. In order to purchase the press we had sold our first house, got a mortgage on our new house, and a second mortgage.

The first name of the company was Research Service Company. It was a terrible name, but anyway that was the name I chose. Getting started was very difficult. I had only two employees, a printer, Wesley Burley, and a bookkeeper by the name of Sullivan. One day the phone rang and it was Claude Owen of the Placement Bureau at Los Angeles City Schools. He stated he had a young man from Indiana who needed work and could I give him a position. I told him I couldn't even feed myself. The answer is 'no.' The first thing I knew Maurice showed up at the office. That was in 1929. I said I had no work for him, but if he wanted to sit out back on a nail keg and paste labels on packages of tests he could.

One very amusing thing is the way Maurice came to get into the accounting business. Sullivan, the bookkeeper, had a very bad habit of getting drunk all the time. One particular morning was pretty bad. He was drunk and lying on the couch in our little reception room. A customer came in and after she left, I said to Sullivan, 'Come into the office. You're fired.' He came into the office and then said a nasty word, and I picked up the telephone and threw it at him. The only reason it didn't kill him was the extension cord wasn't long enough. He ran. I still remember the look on Maurice Wilson's face and Burley's when I came in from chasing Sullivan down the alley. I said to Wilson, 'Do you want to be a bookkeeper?' As a result an auditor from the city schools came out at night and coached him. That's how Maurice got into the accounting work.

Maurice Wilson was a quiet, shy man who worked very hard and was a dedicated worker. He stayed with Ethel for over 40 years. No one could have been more faithful.

Ethel's original intention was just to print tests. However, in order to keep things going, she was determined to increase the family income, so she aggressively pursued other ways to bring in money. To stay in business, she took on letterpress work, printing stationery, business cards, brochures, and posters for small businesses. Among Willis's contacts were people who wanted to have published the educational aids they had prepared. So Ethel began to develop a small catalog of those educational materials in addition to the tests.

Meanwhile Little June, or LJ, the sobriquet my parents dubbed me with, was playing a role in the development of the company too. I became of special interest to Willis as a convenient subject for a variety of testing experiments, ranging from eye-hand coordination to test item selection. Since his natural interest was in child development, he and Ethel had agreed upon a child obedience program that, as I recall, consisted of many, many "no-noes" and incorporated a "let the punishment fit the crime" motif.

A good example of the obedience plan in action involved a cookie and Mrs. Doud when I was about 3. Mrs. Doud was a lovely lady who lived exactly across the street from the Clark home. The Clark home had a little side porch on which I would sometimes sit, and Mrs. Doud would call over little words of cordiality. Now one of the no-noes was a rule stating that I was never, ever to cross the street without Ethel or Willis in hand. One day Mrs. Doud called over as usual, but this time she announced she had just baked some cookies, and if I would come over, I could have one. Well, what was I to do? Willis was working, Ethel was elsewhere, and the cookie was waiting. So I toddled across the street, procured the cookie, toddled back, and ate it. Okay so far. Big mistake ahead: I told Ethel about the cookie. Ethel told Willis. They both became agitated and concerned about my act of willful disobedience. Willis said, "Well, if she's going to run away like a dog, she should get treated like one." So they did so. They got hold of the leash that belonged to Homer (my shivery, shy, sniffly Boston Bull Terrier) and put it on me. They took me into the bedroom, hooked the other end to the bed leg, and told me to stay, which I did. Even worse, they took Mrs. Doud to task about what happened—no more cookies.

Willis also broadened my education by practical lessons in adding and subtracting, which were mostly done on his lap with chips while he was playing poker at the Clarks' habitual Saturday night games. This turned into a very good way to learn, as I had to distinguish the color of the chips, associate the monetary value with the color, and learn to make change.

When I was about 7, he took me to an operetta, "No, No, Nanette" (the "no-no" sounded familiar). Later he took me on a wonderful occasion to a real opera, "Lucia de Lammermoor," with the memorable Lily Pons. Ethel was not interested in opera, so this particular evening was made even more precious because Willis and I had dinner together at a real restaurant. When we were about to leave, thrifty little me spotted some money that Willis had accidentally left under his plate. I gathered it up and raced down after him announcing clearly, "Daddy, you left some money there." I couldn't understand why people were laughing.

Tallying results was another way I learned to help my father. He was very fond of rolling dice to test random sampling; although I didn't understand at that time why he did it so often, I enjoyed keeping the lists for him. Later on I would help him with tallies on tryout test results. Eventually I came to understand that he was testing for probability by random sampling. My father would take a penny that, of course, has two sides, a head and a tail. One would expect that if the penny were tossed a hundred times the probability would be that 50% would be heads and 50% would be tails. However, if the outcome is different, there is reason to think the coin has a defect; that is, perhaps one side is thicker than the other. This thinking could be related to rolling dice. One die could be altered or loaded to change the outcome of a throw and affect the outcome of a game of craps. When Willis found defects like this, he would try to outsmart the "house" by stacking the two dice in such a way that the toss would be more likely to come up a "7" (the lucky number) than if he hadn't stacked them. He would sit and practice for hours.

When I was in the first grade at Normandie Avenue School, I was made Queen of the May. It may have been more than a little coincidence that Willis was then Director of Research for the city schools. Ethel bought me a pretty white dress and found a lovely, little wicker basket, which she filled with those sweet, little Cecile Brunner climbing roses that smell like honey. I walked into the playground of the school and climbed some steps to a little platform to watch the performances and acts of the other children. There was a maypole dance with all the colorful, long ropes, which were woven in and out as the dancers bent down and around to medieval music. It was a lovely, heady day for me, one I never forgot. I think about it every time I see those charming pink miniature roses.

Willis did not simply appreciate me for my willingness to help with the testing. He became a doting father and enjoyed taking me with him to many places. One afternoon he took me to my grandparents' house to see their garden. It was filled with a variety of fruits and vegetables. Undoubtedly he had not forgotten his days as a farmer in South Dakota. There was a fig tree in the midst of this array that had fruit ripening on its branches. Willis picked one and then gave one to me. He bit into his fig and began rolling his eyes, enjoying the treat. He told me to bite into mine. After I did, he said, "Doesn't that feel just like a bunch of ants are crawling around in your mouth?" It was a very long time before I could even look at a fig again.

The Clark family was not very involved in church. My ecclesiastical experience related to Sunday mornings when Willis and Ethel were usually involved in recovering from a hangover, so they would send me off to Sunday school. This was a time when the house was not at its best. I would awaken to the smell of alcohol wafting through the house. I would leave my room in the morning to find empty glasses and liquor bottles on tables. I had received instructions not to touch anything. Why would I? The smell was offensive, and I did not enjoy living in those conditions.

There were many Sundays when either Ethel or Willis would lay out a nickel or a dime for the collection plate when it was passed around. Sunday school was rather fun because I got to color the pages printed with outlines of the various biblical characters. I had to pass a little grocery store on the way to church and again on the way home. One Sunday while walking back home from the church I stopped in. I did not tell the proprietor, although he might well have guessed, that the nickel I had in my pocket to buy some candy was really intended for a higher purpose. Later on I became obsessed with guilt for my breach of duty and should have confessed to my parents, but I didn't.

Willis was a member of the Order of Masons. He would talk to me about the importance of the Masonic order. At least that's what I thought it related to. He often talked about whether one should or should not believe in God and would point out that whether one did or did not, one had to admit that there was some sort of a cohesive purpose that could keep the solar system in its orderly scheme. The regularity of the passing seasons was other evidence of some superior force. This made a very big impression on me, and I would envision the planets as hanging down from the ceiling by strings in such a way that they created their own solar system. Another thing that Willis was very explicit about was the balance of nature. He would give illustrations about the interdependency of all things, a concept that never left me.

Life at the Clark household took a dramatic change when Ethel decided to move the business. From the bungalow in mid-Los Angeles near Normandie and Vernon, she moved west to a business location on Beverly Boulevard near La Brea. The new home was a little larger and had three bedrooms, two baths, a living room, a dining room, a kitchen, a breakfast nook, a back porch, and a basement, which was a feature not often seen in Los Angeles houses. It was in a convenient location, close to buses for transportation and just a few feet from the alley behind Ethel's business, which made it easy for me to report in when coming home from Melrose Avenue School.

Ethel was starting to come into her element. She was devoting more time to the business, so one of the necessary changes was that she no longer had time for cooking, housework, washing, and other chores that she considered were stealing time from running the business. She hired a sequence of helpers to do those chores. There were many notable episodes regarding the persons she hired to help, and two in particular stand out. In one episode, one of the cooks was asked to prepare a vegetable salad and did so out of raw lima beans—goodbye cook. Another episode had to do with a tragic incident in which the lady doing the housekeeping and cooking caught her hand in the washing machine wringer. She became hysterical and was unable to extract it, not thinking to press the emergency release. Sadly—goodbye washing lady—and she was the one who made those good coconut cakes with the seven-minute frosting!

Willis liked to experiment, especially since he was able to put his interest in chemistry to use. These were the infamous days of prohibition, and there were many who felt that their inalienable rights to food and drink were being abused by the government. The 18th Constitutional Amendment was not generally obeyed in the Clark household. Willis decided to obtain some recipes for gin, wine, and beer and use the basement as his laboratory; that is, except for gin, which was made in the manner of the Roaring Twenties, conjuring up the glamorous images of flapper girls and speakeasies.

In reality, bathtub gin was nothing as glamorous as the era portrayed. It was the end result of cheap grain alcohols and flavorings such as juniper berries that were allowed to steep in a tub for several hours or even days. Since the law specifically prohibited the sale or manufacture of distilled alcohol, many producers of bathtub gin were forced to use denatured alcohol that may or may not have been thoroughly processed. A number of partygoers died during the 1920s after drinking contaminated bathtub gin. Willis, through some of his contacts with local educational and political functionaries, was able to get his hands on distilled alcohol, so no one was in danger of being poisoned. That was the good news. The bad news was that it was my bathtub that was used for the process. It was not a happy time for me with the smell of juniper berries permeating my room and the whole house.

It may have been the excitement of bending the law making gin that prompted the desire for another experiment. This time it was beer, with Willis as the biermeister. The scene of the infraction was the basement. It was not my favorite place to be. It was dimly lit and, with its dank smells, reminded me of a creepy, crawly place and brought to mind the book *The Spider and the Fly*, which contained that infamous line "'Will you walk into my parlor?' said the Spider to the Fly." Willis had purchased many big crocks and pots, along with tubes and a large supply of bottle caps. It was my job to affix the tops of the bottles by means of a sort of crimping apparatus. This created a sloppy, stinky mess. After a certain time, the bottles were removed to the garage for safe, secretive keeping. The house aroma bordered on a yeasty, gin-beer fragrance, although that subsided after the beer was moved and after the bathtub gin became so awful to drink that it was dumped from its big porcelain container and subsequently flowed into the Pacific Ocean.

One night a terrible explosion hit our home with intense crackles and pops and very scary noises like shattering glass. "Oh no!" yelled Willis. "Oh goddamn it to hell! Willis, I told you so!" screamed Ethel. That was the end of the alcohol experimentation period.

CHAPTER 6

EXPANSION

In 1929 the superintendent of schools from San Diego came to see Ethel with some important news for her. He pointed out that 75% of the state's school population was in Southern California. Most textbooks were required by law to go into a depository at a fixed price, and, at that time, they were distributed from a depository located in San Francisco. That meant that the southern part of the state, ordering from a depository in San Francisco, was paying about 5% more in transportation charges on the same books used in Northern California. The superintendent convinced Ethel that this was a needed opportunity. In Ethel's words, "That is how the Southern California School Book Depository got started." It was incorporated in 1930. The original capitalization of the company amounted to $25,000. "The way I obtained the money I went to friends at USC, Occidental College, etc. Each put up a little money until we got a total capitalization of $25,000 and we were in business. At least I was. Willis was by then in the Los Angeles City schools as Director of Research and not in my business venture."

The little test business was bringing in a small income that was increasing slowly and ignored by everyone except Willis. Whenever he could garner some spare time, he worked intently on perfecting and developing his test theory. He now had a colleague, Ernest W. Tiegs, Ph.D., who taught educational statistics at the University of Southern California. Together it was their goal to publish "comprehensive" tests designed for the dual purpose of facilitating educational measurement and individual diagnosis, and so the *California Achievement Tests* came into being, metamorphosed from Willis's *Progressive Achievement Test* that was published in 1933.

When Ethel incorporated the schoolbook depository, she was focused on the need for capital to buy equipment and didn't think much in the realm of stocks and stockholders. One of the original purchasers of stock was Dr. William Campbell, a professor at USC. An insidious problem began when he and his wife divorced, and his wife, Emma, acquired the stock under the settlement agreement. Emma made Ethel's life a living hell. She was a heckler and would periodically appear at the office demanding to see "this report and that report." She insisted that no one in the corporation be paid more than $200 a month and similar actions. She would call Ethel at the office or at home, always demanding to see the books and taking up hours of time. Ethel was furious with the situation and would almost have apoplexy whenever Emma called.

Willis found out somehow that Emma was a professional heckler, always filing lawsuits against corporations in which she owned stock. Answering lawsuits is very costly, so rather than a long drawn out battle, Ethel felt she should follow the steps many corporations took to handle these kinds of nuisances. This meant offering Emma a buyout price considerably over the value just to get rid of her. Emma accepted the offer, but the corporate lawyer slipped up and forgot to include a clause by which she would be prohibited from ever buying company stock again. Emma went right out and bought additional shares in the company and started the harassment all over again. Ethel almost went berserk. It wasn't until the company issued Class B shares prohibiting the sale of stock without first offering them to the shareholders, that Emma was persuaded for a goodly price to give up her Class A stock, which could be sold to anyone for Class B stock. Emma made out like the bandit she was, but at last the company was rid of her.

Ethel soon found out the schoolbook depository business was a more time-consuming and costly business than she originally anticipated. First, there were all those books coming in and no place to put them. She moved from her small Beverly Boulevard location into a Bekins storage building located about a mile away on Highland Avenue. She immediately needed to hire a staff, as she needed people to help warehouse, pack, and ship the books to schools throughout Southern California. More staff were needed to take school requests for bids on orders and look up each of those titles in the huge W. K. Bowker compendiums, which listed every book ever printed and its retail price. The costs were then entered on the bid sheets and mailed back to the requesting school district. When the actual orders were received, they were filled, shipped, and the school district billed.

Even I was drafted into walking to the warehouse after junior high school each day to help with compiling the bids and sometimes typing them. They had to be manually typed since there were no computers to simplify and speed things along. Today the faithful Maurice Wilson would be called a financial manager; back then he was called a bookkeeper. He had charge of the billing operation while I did filing under his direction. Maurice was a very quiet man who resembled George Raft, a popular movie star of that era. He told me that filing invoices was a lot like being an ant, "You pick up an invoice and take it and put it in the proper folder. Then go back and pick up another invoice and put it in the proper folder, and then go back and pick up another invoice and put it in the proper folder, and then keep doing it until the job is done."

It was a lot to ask of a twelve-year-old girl, but, nevertheless, I dived in, enjoying the fact that the chores assigned to me made me an integral part of the business while I worked side by side with my mother. I came to realize my family was quite different from the families of my friends. I learned to turn work into play since I had to spend so much time there.

The bidding chore became so voluminous that the bulky W. K. Bowker compendiums that listed book prices became a large part of the Clark lifestyle. They were even taken along on "vacation" to Yosemite National Park. Tables were set up outside the tents. I recall we watched the beautiful Merced River flow by while we looked up prices and prepared bids. Often during the vacation we took what we began to call "Bowker breaks," which added a semblance of fun looking up prices for the prepared bids.

I loved the Yosemite vacations, so I quickly adjusted to being sent to camp in the summertime. Camp became one of my biggest and most anticipated pleasures. Willis got me into the Campfire Girls, who sponsored two camps that served the Los Angeles area: one in the San Bernardino Mountains, called Camp Yallani; and the other, Camp Temescal, in the Santa Monica Mountains, with a path that led from the camp itself to nearby Santa Monica Beach.

At camp I found myself with the companionship of many other children my age. Back at home the Clarks lived in a remote area. I was an only child without many playmates who lived nearby. I was as eager to get to camp each year as my parents were to have me go. They were both still working, of course, and this relieved them of having to take care of me. There were times when I believed my parents were pushing me away, but realistically I understood how busy they were. It was just that they were so eager for me to go to camp that I wondered if somewhere in the annual message of "have a good time at camp" there was an implied "and leave us alone."

There was a girl named Eunice, a year younger than me, who came to camp from Alhambra, California. She was livelier than the children I was used to being around, and her frenetic energy was contagious. Eunice often got me to attempt things I would never have dared. She was smaller than I was but had the coordination to excel at games and sports. She never minded that I was a step slower or didn't have the same physical skill levels she had. Those things never bothered her. She had so much self-assurance during games that she participated for the sheer pleasure of the activity. How anyone else was doing didn't matter to her. She liked that I had read more than she had, so she was eager to learn about the books I had read and why I liked them. She even asked me to make a reading list for her. We bunked in the same cabin and became "buddies" during swim time. Often the college-age counselors who served as lifeguards blew a whistle and water activity came to a halt. Buddies had to grasp hands over their heads while a count was taken to make sure everyone was still above water. I was delighted when Eunice returned the following year, and we renewed our camp relationship as if there had been no time away.

During those times at camp I became more and more interested in nature, becoming proficient in plant identification. Tree climbing was a very big treat and some of the sycamore trees in the Santa Monica area were perfectly shaped for wonderful climbs. They could also be used as hideouts. At Camp Yallani I marveled at the little pine trees and how they clustered in round circles and grew as a group. There were times when I was lucky enough to find such a grouping of trees, and I would go hide in them. The Santa Ana River ran by Camp Yallani. I discovered that I could take a wooden box, remove its bottom, place

31

the box in the shallows of the river, and look through into the water to see all sorts of aquatic life, even baby trout.

With so many days and nights at camp, I got to know many of the songs the girls loved to sing. It was a big event in my camp "career" when I was allowed to serve as song leader, and many of the songs are still with me today. I probably drove Ethel and Willis crazy with my continual reference to and singing of various songs.

The return home from camp was often a sad event. It meant getting back to the same dreary household routine with almost no one around to converse with. Sometimes the various housekeepers and cooks would take me under their wing to show me how to cook certain dishes, how to make the bed properly with hospital corners, and other uninteresting chores.

One time on my return from camp, I expected to be greeted by eagerly awaiting parents, with, perhaps, even a celebratory dinner to mark the happy occasion. Instead the atmosphere in the house when I came in was palpably unfriendly, for Ethel and Willis must have had a fight right before my arrival. The dinner I had looked forward to turned out to be a can of corned beef hash that Ethel had mixed with some corn and almost threw on the table.

"Where's father?" I asked. My mother never answered, just turned and left the room, leaving me alone at the kitchen table with a meal more suited for a prisoner returning from a day on the chain gang than for a child who was eagerly looking forward to a homecoming. I had no idea where my father was, and, though I usually enjoyed his company at the dinner table, I didn't want him around me that evening. My disappointment was a heavy cloud hanging over the table. The anticipation of excitedly relating my camping experiences was lost in another one of their clashes. In the days that followed my return, neither parent asked me anything about camp. It was almost a week before my father asked me how camp had been. I began to tell him but stopped in mid-sentence. I looked at him, fell silent, and went to my room. I still could have told him how camp had been, but what was the point?

This scenario drove home to me the fact that during all the years I went to camp I never received a visit from my parents. I excused my parents' non-visits by rationalizing that the camps were a long way from Hollywood. Yet it was simply making excuses for them on my part because so many other parents made the trip. Nonetheless, my grandparents managed to visit two or three times. I went to camp from when I was 8 until I was 15. At that age I would have had to become a counselor in order to return again. Perhaps at 15 it was time to forsake those pleasant days at camp and the alternate life I had built for myself and return to the life Ethel was building for me. However, I never forgot my days at camp and wondered whether Eunice returned and found a new friend to be her swimming "buddy."

CHAPTER 7

O'BRIEN FROM ALASKA

Sometime in the early 1930s the Clarks decided to take an Alaskan Inside Passage cruise. I went along with them. The small ship stopped at the little towns along the route, ending up at Haines, Alaska, the location of the Chilkoot Barracks of the United States Army. Ethel and Willis spent time there, and, though nothing much was said about it, they apparently liked the place very much. It wasn't too long after our return home that Ethel began talking about a return trip; about Jim O'Brien, whom they had met there; and about an opportunity for Willis (who was a good shot) to go bear hunting with some of the fellows from the barracks. Had I thought about it at the time, I would have realized that this solicitous caring for Willis's interest was a very un-Ethel like turn of events. Anyway, as usual, Ethel got her way and the trip happened. Willis made arrangements for me to be transferred to a school near my grandparents, where I was to stay for the duration, and off they went. Willis actually shot a black bear. He had it made into a rug with its mouth wide open. At certain times, when the light was right, it terrified me.

The real story remains clouded. However, I believe Ethel was quite taken with O'Brien, but I was too young at the time to recognize the signs. I believe Ethel maneuvered work schedules so they could go back to Alaska. While Willis was out hunting bear, she and O'Brien could get to know each other better.

Sadly it was not only a bear that they came back with. Shortly thereafter Ethel was taken very seriously ill; so ill, in fact, that she developed peritonitis and suffered cruelly. Willis never mentioned anything about the details of Ethel's condition to me, although he knew I was aware of how ill Ethel was. Willis had to hire household help to care for me and to cook and perform other household duties. Ethel's screams could be heard all over the neighborhood, and morphine seemed to be the only antidote that would help. Neighbors would drop by with food, and one time our next-door neighbors took me in for several nights. Their daughter and I were good friends, and as the parents spoke only Italian, it was an adventure for me, but I was terrified when I heard Ethel's screams. It was a horrible period and all but a miracle that she survived.

In later years, perhaps feeling the need for some sort of explanation, Ethel told me that while Willis was out hunting bear, she was left alone and was raped by some terrible man who burst into the tent when she had nothing with which to defend herself. In the mid-1960s, Ethel sent me a letter addressed "To my only child (the other child died!)." Naturally this led to all sorts of speculation, casting doubts on the story of her being raped. It was well within Ethel's character to have manipulated the trip so she could pursue her infatuation with O'Brien.

Jim O'Brien was the prototypical Alaskan one imagines when thinking of that vastly undeveloped state back in the 1930s. He was big, ruggedly handsome, self-sufficient, a risk taker (think of John Wayne and the correct image will come into your head), who had eked out a living under extremely adverse conditions. In short, he was everything Willis wasn't. O'Brien obviously saw Ethel, with her movie star good looks, as the most desirable woman he had seen in years. When they were together one could warm one's hands from the sparks flying between them. Willis, however, content to be enjoying his nights of poker with the men at the barracks, surely didn't notice. When Ethel suggested a return trip for more hunting, poker, and drinking with the guys, Willis probably jumped at the opportunity to distance himself for a while from the tedium of working with numbers and statistics, no matter how much he loved his work.

Any B-movie scriptwriter could place them in some rustic cabin in the wilds of Alaska—say on a bitterly cold night—with a crackling fire, Jack Daniels, and enough time to have the camera slowly fade from the bedroom of the dimly lit cabin to a raging snowstorm outside with drifts piling up alongside the cabin walls. Any B-movie scriptwriter, or even I, could have written that scenario after reading the letter Ethel sent me in the 1960s.

Did she have an illegal abortion and develop peritonitis, or less likely, did she have a miscarriage that probably would not have left her so terribly ill? It is very plausible that this event was the start of the coolness between Willis and Ethel. Although they had a growing business to keep them together, that wonderful feeling of warmth between them was gone. Perhaps this was a scar of guilt that, along with her bodily scar, Ethel carried for those many years.

Things seemed to go well after Ethel's recovery. I was getting good grades in school, the new depository location was working out, and Willis's dream of a simulated case history for every pupil was taking shape. However, Ethel began to develop a condition that caused her to be allergic to the sun and to develop miserable itchy rashes. Summers in Los Angeles can get very hot from a relentless sun, tempered somewhat by eye-burning, stifling smog. This was all but unbearable for Ethel. The Clarks searched for, found, and rented a beach house in the Malibu area where it was cooler, and Ethel stayed out of the sun as much as possible. Willis still had to go to work almost every day, but Ethel would go infrequently, relying on a couple of trusted employees to manage to keep things going. It was about then that the thought of a second home in a cooler location took hold.

CHAPTER 8

SURGE

In the 1930s a tremendous surge in the testing business began along with the growth of the schoolbook depository, so once more Ethel was forced to look for larger quarters. She found them in midtown Los Angeles at the American Storage Company building at 3636 Beverly Boulevard. A bus very close to the Clark residence went straight to the storage building, so it was too convenient to pass up.

It was a major move, since along with employees, the move involved presses, cutters, linotypes, and bindery equipment. Of course thousands and thousands of books needed to be warehoused. It was a huge building with high ceilings and racks and racks of sturdy metal shelving to hold the heavy books. It was a mess when the move was made. Books were stored in boxes and on large wooden tables until they could be organized and properly placed on the shelves. It took tremendous amounts of man-hours to accomplish this task, but under Ethel's supervision it was done. She knew exactly how she wanted everything for maximum efficiency. The building was big enough to accommodate everything and everyone.

There was a convenient little half-hidden alcove behind the elevator on the third floor. This alcove became a spot for the testing business to be conducted. Eventually, with the advent of the test-scoring machine, there was even a sign pointing to what the burgeoning testing business was beginning to be called: The California Test Bureau.

An elevator that opened into the warehouse on the third floor should have been a convenience but was the cause of some confusion. When people got off the elevator, they were confronted by the hundreds of shelves from the schoolbook depository bulging with books and other educational materials. The little sign indicating CTB's location was easy to overlook, so CTB customers could be found wandering in a daze, lost in the morass. It was not just the customers that were lost as the building was open to everyone. So salespeople, repairmen, and employees could be found in the mix along with beggars looking for handouts.

One day the famous movie star, Eva Gabor, accidentally wandered into the building. She was dressed very stylishly in a white satin dress that flared out from her hips into a wide skirt. She wore a matching wide-brimmed hat and was carrying a Pekingese dog and a white sun umbrella. She also had a small entourage following her, so it was impossible not to notice her. No one remembers what she was looking for. She was obviously in the wrong building. Nonetheless, she created a momentary diversion for the employees.

One test customer had a terrible experience when she encountered a very ugly panhandler who was an amputee and got in her face demanding money. The man was very scruffy and moved about with the assistance of a crutch. When she refused him money, he yelled at her and said, "I hope to God you have something like this happen to you so you know how I feel." That episode prompted Ethel to have a desk placed by the elevator with a lady stationed there to direct traffic. Having an employee stationed by the elevator just to direct traffic was a very inefficient use of the employee's time. Ethel was not going to tolerate wasted time, so until she could get the storage company management to install a more appropriate sign, she had the lady score tests.

It was also about this time that something happened to trigger the interest of the IRS in the schoolbook depository and CTB. It had to do with the methods used to handle the warrants that came in from school districts in lieu of payments and how they were recorded, processed, and reported that resulted in some kind of mix-up. Ethel knew better than to try to handle the situation herself so she transferred the contacts and explanations to a certified public accountant. However, she was really not ready to let the situation run its normal course because she was outraged to have to spend time and money on a review of documents and to suffer such an invasion of the company's interests.

She did not believe the company owed any back taxes. Besides, she was not about to succumb to the intimidation procedures the IRS used to scare people into compliance and cooperation with their auditors, so she did not want their job to be an easy or comfortable one. The IRS audit took place in the middle of summer during a brutal Los Angeles hot spell. The night before the investigators were to appear, Ethel had a few employees set up heaters in the designated room and told them to let them run all night. She had them removed right before the meeting. By the end of the day, the auditors looked like they had been in a steam room. No action was taken against the company since the IRS concluded there was some confusion in bookkeeping that was not intentional.

Ethel was not the kind of woman who associated with other women. She had very few female employees in the company and almost no personal female friends. One exception was her cousin, Helen, who was a very attractive, outgoing person. Helen was one of the few in Ethel's limited circle of women whose looks could compete with her own. She did not particularly like her cousin. She thought she was a bit of a flirt, but she was her cousin, so she tolerated her as she and her husband often came over to the Clarks to play poker. When the husband fell on hard times, Helen asked Ethel for a job. Ethel reluctantly made room for her at the Bekins Storage Company location doing filing and other tasks. At the same time Helen was doing the filing, a very attractive man named David was handling billing, which required a lot of filing. One can be distracted easily when filing and perhaps Helen found the job tedious. Place an attractive woman in a boring job with time on her hands, throw in a good looking man, and you can sit back and watch the sparks fly.

I came over after school one day to find Helen sobbing and Ethel screaming at her to "Get out!" Apparently Ethel had gone looking for David. She had opened the door to his office to find David handling Helen as well as the billing. Such behavior could not be tolerated, so who could blame Ethel for going into a rage, calling Helen nasty names. She did not care who heard her rant, which became a public dressing down and tarnishing of Helen's reputation. It was the end of what had been a nice friendship and reinforced Ethel's belief that women are not to be trusted. She did not excuse David's behavior—he was ordered to leave too. However, Ethel was much harder on Helen than she was on David.

CHAPTER 9

DEVOTED INTERLOPER

Around 1930 an event took place that was to affect our family forever. It is still a mystery to me how it happened, but suddenly our family of three became a family of four—just like that! This is Ethel's version of what happened:

> About that time a wonderful person came into our life. To show you how crazy the Clarks are, we take in stray humans, stray animals, anything that's in trouble. One of our high school principals [Ralph Person] came by one afternoon bringing Warren Hook with him. They were only there about 15 minutes. A few weeks later this principal started calling about this poor Warren Hook who was sick and destitute. Finally it got so bad Willis said, "I can't stand this, let's go over and see." So we got the car out, and the result was that we loaded Warren into the back seat of the car and took him home with us. I took the dogs out of the extra room they had been using and put Warren to bed there. The doctor said he had pneumonia and was too weak to be moved into a hospital. There was only one thing to do—take care of him. So we took care of him. He was in bed six months. I kept saying to Willis, I know he's going to ask for a job.
>
> Warren did ask for work and he started working in the shipping department. He came to accept us as his family and lived with us 27 years. My mother and father worshiped him. He would baby-sit with June while we went dancing, and later on he took on the grandchildren. When he died

suddenly in 1956 from a heart attack it shook the entire family. He died on Thanksgiving Day of 1956 at Pebble Beach and is buried here on the Peninsula. He spent every penny of his salary on June or on the grandchildren. His hobbies were gardening, photography and tinkering around cars with my dad.

The book depository business became so competitive that I began to receive threatening calls warning me to get out of the business. There was an incident where I felt that Warren actually saved my life. One day a threatening call demanding I get out of the depository business was received. It was the usual stuff, 'don't come downstairs or you're going to get killed,' etc. I paid no attention to it because I believed my competitors were only trying to throw a scare into me. Warren had at that time an old car with windshield wipers that didn't work. It was in the month of February and it was pouring rain. I came downstairs after receiving another threatening phone call, got in my car which was parked out in front, slid over to the side to drive home at which time another car came right up alongside me. I can't describe it except all of a sudden the door of my car opened and there was this gun in my side. By that time, Warren had driven out of the parking lot and had come around and his headlights went right on the scene. The men, whoever they were, drove away. Warren went after them, as he had seen what was happening. He chased them for blocks, up and down streets but lost them. When he came back to me, I had gone into shock. I was frozen with fear. I was sitting there and I couldn't talk. He drove me home. He called the doctor. I still couldn't talk. I'd been overworked. I had worked night and day so many years trying to make something of the companies. So the doctor suggested that I be taken out of town if my life was endangered. Mr. Hook was given a gun permit and ordered not to let me out of his sight. It took me almost six months to overcome the shock of this experience.

41

That was when Warren Hook became firmly entrenched in the Clark household. He had saved Ethel's life and was a hero. He was suddenly indispensable. He was tall and blond and had been captain of the football team at the University of Hawaii but, most unfortunately, broke his back during play. How all this translated to a permanent home with the Clarks is still somewhat of a mystery that was never made clear to me, but there he was. The three of them—Ethel, Willis, and Warren—went everywhere together. It is not unusual for the head of a company, a legislator, or a political figure to need someone to serve as an intermediary or in a protective capacity; Warren, with Ethel's grooming, assumed that role. She taught Warren how to dress successfully. He learned manners from her and easily grew into his role as Ethel's right-hand man. He became a very polished and formidable person. His position changed as time went on. Warren did whatever Ethel asked of him. There was no task too menial or too difficult for him to tackle. He performed everything with diligence and devotion to Ethel that resembled the behavior of a puppy rescued from the dog pound.

Warren eventually assumed the title of Vice-President, but his major and ongoing role seemed to be that of a buffer. Warren stepped in if there was something or someone that Ethel wished to avoid, with that role constantly expanding as Ethel began to distance herself from anything that irritated her or took valuable time away from running the business. He became her acting spokesperson when needed, running interference with the skills accumulated during his days as a football player. When she needed something, which was quite often, he was always there to fetch it. He began to anticipate her needs. "Her wish was his command" was the cliché that suited him perfectly. His transition from the business side to the social and family side was accomplished so smoothly that it was simply a fait accompli that all of us accepted almost without question. I certainly didn't question it because there was no apparent resistance from Willis, who continued to immerse himself in developing tests.

My own recollections and feelings are not easily disguised. As a child, my feelings were fairly neutral because of my lack of understanding. I remember that one day Warren showed up and simply stayed on, and on, and on. Ethel's explanation of helping someone in need was so out of character for her mainly because she and Willis had so many other time commitments. It made no sense they would take on a friend of a friend who had pneumonia. Through the years there were certain things I had to come to terms with about my mother. It is more likely that Warren was one of Ethel's many loves—perhaps the most difficult thing I've had to come to terms with. I think she had an immediate attraction for him and decided to follow through with her own desires and bring him to the house. If Ethel's behavior was difficult for me to understand, Willis's was completely baffling to me. He shared the same bedroom with Ethel, but if he had anything to say about the situation, he kept it to himself. You cannot imagine the power of Ethel's personality—if she wanted something, she went after it until she got it.

I viewed Warren as an absolute toady. There was nothing he wouldn't do for my mother. She said "do it" and he did it. His only form of rebellion was to sneak smokes whenever he could. I was tempted to rat him out but never did. Ethel was dead set against smoking. It is amazing she never caught Warren lighting up. He would hide in the bushes, or if he saw me coming, he had a way of curling up the cigarette in his hand so it couldn't be seen, or so he thought, as if he could hide the smoke coming from it.

I recall an incident when I thought Warren showed a streak of cruelty that was unusual for him. Ethel had a Filipino man who cooked and drove for her. He lived in a comfortable room off the kitchen in the Hollywood Hills house. He did something while driving Ethel that made her suspicious of his driving skills. She asked Warren to check his driver's license, and if it wasn't in order, to help him obtain another one. Warren discovered the license was horribly out of date. He tore it up and told the driver to get another one. The driver could barely speak English, and tearing up his driver's license was tantamount to taking away his means of making a living. He went berserk. He was so angry we actually feared for our lives. Ethel had the knives removed from the kitchen. She eventually had Warren call the police, and I never knew what happened to him except he was gone from our household. He had been driving illegally, but Warren didn't have to tear up his license.

It was an interesting and volatile time in the history of the country. Things were moving quickly in both New York and Hollywood. After the stock market crash of 1929, *Variety* reported "Wall Street Lays an Egg." The Depression enveloped the country in hard times as millions of Americans found themselves without jobs and without places to live. There was, however, one place that seemed immune to the Great Depression—Hollywood, where the young movie industry was turning out moneymaking films that boomed the economy on the West Coast.

Billy Wilkerson was a young speakeasy operator who arrived in Hollywood in 1930. He thought a western version of the trade journal *Variety* was needed, so he launched his new tabloid *The Hollywood Reporter*. At first the executives from the movie studios were opposed to Wilkerson's paper because it often criticized the industry. However, they soon realized that any publicity was good publicity and that reporting on the goings-on of their movie stars in the various nightclubs springing up around Los Angeles was very good for business. The studios began depicting scenes in nightclubs with lavish settings in their movies. Cigarette girls wandered among the elegantly dressed patrons. Camera girls snapped pictures of the patrons and delivered the photos directly to the table while they enjoyed the entertainment. Beautiful chorus girls and the lives of glamorous stars were welcome distractions for a nation with little to be cheerful about. Movies became an escape from the realities of hard economic times and a way for the average person to spend a few hours in a darkened theater, where the realities of their lives could be left outside on the sidewalk.

One of the most popular places to see and be seen was the Coconut Grove. The Ambassador Hotel converted the grand ballroom into a nightclub that attracted all the famous movie stars of the day as well as the social elite of the city. Stars like Sophie Tucker and Bing Crosby would sing to a packed house. Ethel wanted to be part of this fast-moving scene. Ethel loved to dance. Willis was not a good dancer and usually avoided having to step on a dance floor. Yet, to accommodate Ethel, he would accompany her to the hot spots such as the Plantation Club in Culver City, which became the center for nightlife.

The Sunset Strip also became a place to be for nighttime excitement. The Strip was a two-mile stretch of Sunset Boulevard between Laurel Canyon Boulevard and Doheny Drive. It symbolized Hollywood glamour. The Beachcomber was a bar and restaurant, outfitted to look like a South Sea island hangout, complete with the sound of rain on the roof. They served exotic rum drinks and Polynesian fare. The Beachcomber became popular with both the Hollywood crowd and the socialites who were able to live movie stars' lives vicariously by hobnobbing with them.

Warren was very presentable, and he was a good dancer. He liked to dress well and was the perfect complement to Ethel on the dance floor, where they would swirl off and leave Willis to contend with me. Willis even tried to teach me to dance, which was not easy for him. Willis had to count as he took each step and look down now and then to be sure his feet were doing what they should.

"Tea dances" were held on weekend afternoons and were very in vogue. The four of us would go to places like the famous Cotton Club in Culver City, where Lionel Hampton, Cab Calloway, and Duke Ellington would play to huge crowds in the late afternoon. Often the musicians were followed by a visit from what we now call "stand up" comedians, whose risqué material was often enhanced by semi-strip teasers. (I never could figure out how the ladies could get their breasts circulating in opposite directions—quite a feat!) There were times when the comedian was billed as a "top banana" and kept things moving at a brisk and lively pace.

Ethel, somewhat desperately, somewhat pathetically, tried to break into this glamorous lifestyle of rubbing elbows with the movie stars by inviting entertainers to our home. Somehow she didn't make the cut with the Hollywood crowd, who always managed to decline her invitations. Even the well-known movie/television personality, Alan Hale, who was a neighbor, never accepted an invitation from Ethel.

Poker was another of Ethel and Willis's favorite pastimes. Warren would drive them to various friends' homes for the games. He became such an acceptable part of the grouping that he would be invited to join. Eventually the invitation always included him. It was inevitable that Ethel and Warren began to be the topic of gossip and innuendo among their social strata, and many of the comments were not very nice, particularly when it became known that Warren rubbed Ethel's feet every evening. There were some who called Warren her second husband but Ethel didn't care; in fact, she relished the situation, knowing full well that it was one more thing that made her different from other women. It was another way she could stretch the envelope. She was competing successfully in a man's world by running a growing company. She was not afraid to take on the challenges of all that her situation entailed. If there was a double moral standard that applied to women, she did not let the implications or the ramifications impede her in any way.

Warren never looked at another woman; perhaps he didn't dare, but there was never any indication that he was anything but totally devoted to Ethel. However one wants to analyze the relationship between Ethel and Warren, it seems apparent that he took the load off Willis. Willis hated shopping, driving, gardening, cooking on the barbecue, and all the little chores that Warren seemed so willing to do. And he did them much better than Willis. I once dared to report others' comments about Warren to Willis, but instead of being outraged, Willis just shrugged and said, "I'm happy with things this way." There are many interpretations that could be attributed to that statement, but, in the end, how can you argue with happiness. Willis was such a private person that it was impossible to know what kind of world he lived in. Whatever that world was, he was content with his life as he never commented, complained, or lamented his state.

Well, that was the Warren situation. Despite what Ethel had said, it was not the dogs that got kicked out of their bedroom with its attached bath—it was me. I remember well Warren taking over my room, and I was pretty upset about it because the bedroom I moved to was much smaller. I don't recall ever being asked my opinion, and no explanation was given as to who Warren was and why he took over my room. My new room abutted the next-door neighbor's driveway, and their kitchen window looked right into my bedroom. I want to go on record as resenting Warren right from the very beginning. I looked upon him as an intruder, and his constant companionship with my mother was a considerable annoyance. It didn't become an embarrassment until I was older and could understand the implications better. It was very difficult for me to accept him as a member of the family, which seemed to be what was expected of me. I think Ethel simply expected me to play my role as the "dumb kid on the block" and become more accepting and understanding. That wasn't the case at all—I never did accept Warren.

It wasn't until after he died in 1956 that I could see another side to him and all the various roles he played in our family dynamics. He was everything from errand boy to grocery shopper, driver, gardener, family photographer, and everything in between. In connection with the business, he became what would best be described as an aide to Ethel. She made her wishes known via Warren, which gave him a sort of power that he could never have achieved on his own. Perhaps Ethel saw and appreciated some kind of strength in him. However, because of his parrot-like involvement in both household and business affairs, I considered him a total wimp, as I perceived that Ethel was capitalizing on his intense devotion. There is no doubt she used it as a control mechanism to keep him in line and at her beck and call.

As far as I know, Ethel and Willis met Warren the first time he and Ralph Person visited them. It is very difficult for me to buy into the fact that without knowing him more than that one brief visit they would load Warren into the back seat of the car and take him to our home and nurse him back to health. I don't remember Warren being ill—why would they take on this burden? They were both working. Even though her business was close by, Ethel had neither the time nor the inclination to care for a sick person. The conclusion I reached many years later was that this was a different rendition of the Alaska episode, in the sense that Ethel had a strong attraction to Warren and decided to go out and get him and bring him back. Willis didn't have much say about anything, or maybe he just plain didn't care, or maybe Ethel sold him some story about why Warren should be there. That song "Whatever Lola Wants, Lola Gets" was appropriate many times over, and Warren might just well have been what she wanted—she could use him to her advantage and did.

Warren even renounced his own family to be with Ethel. Her insistence on total loyalty was so adamant that she didn't want his family interfering with her relationship with Warren, and, because of her strong will, she didn't want her own family interfering with it either. Warren did not communicate with his sister and his parents, who had a dairy in Upland, California. They kept trying to reach him, but he acceded to Ethel's wishes and pushed them aside. I don't recall why, but one day we went to Upland to visit his folks. The tension was almost visible with the naked eye and so palpable that one could feel it. I remember that for dinner we had buttered bread and milk—that was it. It was some contrast to the lobster and steak fare we had at home when company came. I imagine the discrepancy in living conditions, plus Ethel's antagonism toward Warren's family brought on by her sense of elitism, prompted his decision to completely break with his family. He even ignored them in his will, which I'll bet Ethel had something to do with because she always insisted that he pay his household debts. She would not have wanted any of his money going to his family.

CHAPTER 10

PLAYING WITH THE BIG BOYS

Willis slowly continued fulfilling his dream of a simulated case history for every pupil. Along the way he became concerned that some of those taking the tests might be inadvertently scored below their actual ability because of problems with seeing, hearing, or the ability to properly hold a pencil. With this in mind he developed three tests: *Pre-Test of Visual Acuity*, *Pre-Test of Auditory Acuity*, and *Pre-Test of Motor Coordination*. He also worried that some children were being unduly pushed into reading when they weren't ready for it, so he and a colleague, D. J. Murray Lee, Chair of the Department of Education at South Illinois University, co-authored what became a very popular test called the *Lee-Clark Reading Readiness Test*. The test was most helpful in identifying children who are at the various stages of preparedness for beginning reading. That in turn led to another collaboration, the *Lee-Clark Arithmetic Fundamentals Survey Test*.

Things were fairly well with the business in the late 1930s. There was an ongoing sense of excitement and accomplishment with the continuing hums and kerplunks of the presses and the clinks from the linotypes on one side of the building, the calling back and forth of the workers in the shipping and handling departments on the other side of the building, and the workers running up and down between floors. Added to that, there was the rumor that a new way to score tests was being developed by International Business Machines (IBM).

In the early 1930s, a teacher, R. B. Johnson, devised for his own use a machine equipped with counters to record student test answers and compare them to an answer key set up on the machine. IBM learned of Johnson's device and hired him in 1934 to develop the original production model of his machine, which could read pencil marks on an examination paper and translate the marks into a visual indication of the total net score. Ethel was receiving calls about her possible interest in buying a machine (they were very expensive) and, in fact, was being directly courted by one of their representatives. IBM announced the Type 805 Test Scoring Machine in 1938. Tests to be scored by the machine were answered by marking spaces on separate answer sheets that had a capacity of 750 response positions, or 150 five-choice questions, or 375 true-false questions. The answer sheets were dropped into the 805 for processing. Getting a test publishing company to endorse the machine would have been a big plus for IBM. Ethel, who had little or no interest in test development and all that it entailed, was all for buying the machine. She felt that the teachers must be bored sitting and hand-scoring all those pages of tests and would welcome this new procedure. The market was there for the trying.

Willis was aghast and voiced his opposition in this manner, "Ethel, you have no idea what you're saying. If the teachers don't hand-score the tests they won't be able to see the mistakes that the kids are making and help them understand and work through their trouble spots. Not only that, we would have to completely reformat the tests so the kids would mark some predetermined answers, recheck all the test items for reliability and validity, and go through a very expensive re-standardization. It would cost a fortune."

Ethel retaliated in a very practical, business-like way, always with an eye towards new technology, "Willis, always watch what the Big Boys are doing. If IBM is willing to come through with the kind of money it took to build and put this machine on the market, I'm willing to buy it." And so it went. There was a great deal of publicity about the machine with all the promised improvements in education and the claim that teachers could spend their time teaching instead of scoring tests.

Once again Ethel got her way and went ahead and bought one of the first test-scoring machines. Willis went to work developing plans on how to reconstruct all his tests. The venture, while eventually paying off, set the company back a lot of money, and the Clarks had to resort to factoring with the bank, which was a very tedious and somewhat scary procedure. In effect what factoring does is to take an organization's accounts receivable as collateral and loan money based on those accounts. Fortunately for Ethel, most all of her receivables were with school districts, and, for the most part, their credit was good.

There were very few that never paid; however, there were some cases where the payments were very long in coming because of a shortage of funds, in which case warrants were usually issued that guaranteed payment at some future time.

The advent of the test-scoring machine in the 1930s instituted a new era of test construction and processing, not just for CTB, but for other test publishers and school districts as well. The machine, compared to today's standards, was out of date before it got started because it was so cumbersome and time consuming. It may have saved teachers' time and patience, but it added frustration and boredom for its operators. From outward appearances the machine looked like a desk with a slit and some knobs on the top. On the right side was a large drawer that could be pulled out and held a platen with lots of little prongs, each of which was capable of making a small electric charge when encountering graphite. The answer sheets, at one time only available from IBM, were marked with a special pencil called an electrographic machine scoring pencil with lead that contained enough graphite to produce a charge. A stencil was overlaid on the platen with only the correct answers showing so that when the answer sheet was inserted into the slot and contact was made, a reading of the number of correct answers showed on the voltmeter on top of the desk. The scores were then hand-marked on the answer sheets. The machine could register only three scores, so if there were more subtests than three, the answer sheet had to be reprocessed so the other subtest scores could be recorded.

The scores obtained were called "raw scores" because to be meaningful they had to be converted into norm-referenced scores. This was all done by hand and was very time consuming, but at least the teachers didn't have to do it. In addition, CTB was developing reports that were helping the teacher help the child.

In the late 1930s the first electrographic machine scoring pencils were manufactured out of metal that accepted long thin strips of lead. The idea was that the students would insert the lead when the existing strip was used up, but as you can imagine, the strips would break and there would be a mess all over the desks and on hands and clothing too. Besides that, they were expensive. However, graphite was essential to making the machine work, so eventually pencils were developed that looked like regular lead pencils, were heavy with graphite, and had special erasers. Ethel saw the value of selling these pencils along with the answer sheets, and the venture became a very profitable combination. Today the scoring technology is much improved, and a #2 pencil serves the same purpose.

Reconstruction of the tests in order for them to be used with answer sheets was a laborious undertaking that Willis headed. Up until then the test questions were printed on the test booklets and the students marked their answers right on the pages. Now all possible and likely (and unlikely) answers needed to be numbered, positioned, and printed in such a way that they could be marked on the answer sheets. Selecting the appropriate answers involved new studies in item selection and extensive analysis to be certain the items maintained their reliability and validity. The following example shows the change in an item from booklet format to format for use with an answer sheet:

Booklet Format:
The longest river in the United States is the _____.

Format for Use with Answer Sheet:
The longest river in the United States is the

a. Missouri

b. Columbia

c. Amazon

d. Mississippi

As is apparent, somewhat different skills are used when the answer selection changes from the student drawing on his/her knowledge from memory and writing in the answer (in the booklet format) to the student selecting the best answer from the preselected choices (in the format for use with an answer sheet). Therefore, intensive work went into perfecting the predetermined responses. The tests had to first undergo what is known as an item tryout in order to ascertain the most appropriate questions for the grade levels of the test. After that the actual item selection was made.

Still later there had to be a completely new standardization, which meant obtaining students from selected school districts throughout the United States, providing the tests and answer sheets to them, getting back the responses and comments, and processing them through recognized statistical methods. This method was used to obtain norms—a very time-consuming, arduous, and expensive task—which could be used for individual assessment and for class and district comparison if a school district so desired.

Ethel continued to consider Willis's concern about the teachers not having access to their students' test scores if they were using answer sheets that had to be sent somewhere to be scored. She ended up taking Willis's concept of the *Diagnostic Analysis of Learning Difficulties*, that identified the specific purpose of each test item, and putting an answer sheet on top of the *Diagnostic Analysis* with a sheet of carbon paper in between. That way when the student took the test and marked the answers on the answer sheet, the mark would carry through onto the *Diagnostic Analysis*, and the teacher could see at a glance which items had been missed and specifically what they were testing. The answer sheet itself could be detached and either hand-scored by the teacher or sent in to be processed.

Ethel wanted a good name for her invention and came up with "SCOREZE," which really said it all. She discovered she could patent the idea and went ahead with the process in 1950, acquiring the patent in her name. There was no doubt she was responsible for the idea, but the tests involved were copyrighted by both Willis and his co-author Dr. Tiegs. It did not matter much to Willis, but Tiegs was furious that she went ahead without getting his permission and was even more furious that he wouldn't receive any royalties from the sale of SCOREZE. Tiegs couldn't believe that the simple insertion of a piece of carbon paper could be patentable. The tension between Ethel and him escalated, with Tiegs threatening to bring a lawsuit against her if she continued, which, of course, she did. The close proximity of their respective office spaces in an already crowded room did nothing to relieve the tension. In the end, Tiegs never did pursue his lawsuit over SCOREZE, but the bitterness stayed with him.

During all this time, Willis was trying to work with Tiegs on developing the next tests scheduled for production.

CHAPTER 11

IN THE MIDST OF CHAOS

In the late 1930s the new venture was going well when rumors of the involvement of the United States in the war in Europe began to spread. There was talk that there would be a draft of young men into the armed forces, and, sure enough, it happened. Even prior to the actual draft, men were enlisting to go overseas to help the Allies, and among those was a handsome linotype operator named Earl. It was with almost total disbelief that very soon after his enlistment and departure we read he had been killed in an aircraft training accident. Apprehension and gloom began to take over the schoolbook depository operations and personnel, which consisted mostly of young men. Patriotism and its glory enveloped the nation, and there was enormous political and personal pressure on all sides to enlist. Dirty glances were given to men not in uniform. It didn't matter that they might have good reasons to stay out of the Army, people just jumped to the conclusion they were "draft dodgers." Also, some Americans had a difficult time distinguishing the various Asian peoples, which led to terrible misunderstandings. A Korean student, who assisted with processing the test-scoring machine, had to have an American flag sewn onto his jacket so he was not mistaken as Japanese and could get to work safely. He was often called bad names and once was accosted as he transferred buses.

One by one, most of the employees either were drafted or moved to some job where they were exempt from the draft. The strain of the long extra hours required of those remaining to keep up with the incoming orders was very difficult to deal with.

That was all bad enough without another great shock that was about to occur—the closing of the schoolbook depository. In a later interview Ethel told the story about this sad event. When she was asked about the demise of the schoolbook depository she said:

> The schoolbook depository was given up when the war came on. I was then in the American Storage Company, which is now owned by the Bell Telephone Company on Beverly Boulevard and Vermont in Los Angeles. The company (CTB) was just beginning to develop. We had a few more tests; we had a big book display in the front room. We had a floor and a half of schoolbooks, textbooks and workbooks. The war came on, the armed forces took over all the larger buildings and we were ordered out and given only 30 days to move 14,800 textbooks plus the presses. We fought like dogs. Mr. Huebner, our attorney, finally got a 60-day extension but we had to move on weekends at double costs. We knew our competitors in the depository business were almost broke. I called them up and told them we were ordered out of the building and did they want to buy the Southern California School Book Depository. There were two partners and they said 'yes.' They agreed that I would pretend to be in business for one year. I was to receive both the orders and the payments. They were to fill the orders from their consigned stock. In that way I was protected. The whole thing ended tragically. After that one year, the purchasers actually did go bankrupt, one partner committed suicide and the other died. Different book companies brought suit against the widows, took everything they had, and then who walked away with our ten years' work but Vroman's Bookstore of Pasadena.
>
> We then had to look for a building to house CTB, but could not find anything big enough. The war was on. The only place we could find was a portion of a building at 5916 Hollywood Boulevard. We went in there in the month of August, and I'm telling you, I sat down in the middle of the floor and cried. Warren was with me. It was a 55 or 60 year-old filthy building at that time. But it had a roof. The toilets had just half a seat on them. There was oil in the floor. There was no ventilation and the heat was unbearable.

> It got so hot in there that we would carry buckets of ice
> water around to try to work and if it got too bad we went
> home. It was terrible.

The task of transforming the dilapidated shambles of the large garage, storage rooms, and sagging offices into a modern plant with up-to-date offices would have been a daunting task for most people, but Ethel had a vision. She used her exceptional powers of persuasion. She found workmen and managed to procure a clean area for the presses, an attractive lobby/reception area, offices facing Hollywood Boulevard, a comfortable meeting room, plus many auxiliary offices and areas for anticipated new equipment. She accomplished all this during the time of short building supplies, gas rationing, and a greatly reduced labor force.

In the middle of the chaos surrounding the sale of the schoolbook depository and the move—that, of course, included the presses and related equipment, the test inventory, shelving, office equipment, and all the other accoutrements—Ethel received word that the *MacQuarrie Test for Mechanical Ability* was being printed and administered by the U.S. Army without permission. This was simply too much for her to absorb considering all that she had been through with the forced evacuation from the storage building, the sale of the schoolbook depository, the loss of money due to the relocation, and the eventual renovation of the garage and offices. She never for a moment entertained the thought of gratuitously or patriotically granting the Army any rights to the test, and Dr. MacQuarrie, the author whose royalties were at stake, certainly agreed. Ethel brought suit against the Army for infringements, loss of revenues, and everything else that could be folded into the claim. The suit was handled by Herbert Huebner, the intellectual property rights attorney who had handled the Emma Campbell affair, and, after eight long, intense years, Ethel won. She was awarded $8,000 and a cease and desist order.

After the war the testing business began to grow by leaps and bounds. Naturally, as more tests were sold, more had to be printed. CTB was doing all of its own printing in the Los Angeles office at that time with the exception of the IBM answer sheets that were printed in Endicott, New York. CTB had quite a large printing establishment and employed a great many people to operate the presses, bindery, and other equipment necessary for making the test booklets. The policy had always been followed of having what is known as an open shop, with the belief that no employee should have to pay for the right to hold a position.

As CTB grew, it became necessary to operate the printing presses as much as twenty-four hours a day. Believe me, it was quite a strain trying to keep the necessary help and the necessary equipment to meet all the customer demands for the tests.

This went on for several years until 1951. Several men walked into Warren Hook's office one afternoon and announced they were union representatives. They had papers for management to sign that would have made our print shop a closed shop. It would have been extremely easy to have just signed the papers, which would have forced every member in the printing department to join the union and start paying dues. It also would have made it necessary for them to join the union if they wanted to keep their jobs. Ethel's reaction compared to a mother tiger protecting her cubs. This is what Ethel had to say about it:

> Well, when I heard of this I really hit the ceiling. You can imagine how I must have felt about some of these employees who had been with me for a number of years and who had done such good work for us. I could not turn traitor on them and force them to join a union. I absolutely refused to sign the union agreements. Union representatives also told us that if we did not sign the papers saying that we would have a closed shop then the printers' union would throw a picket line around our offices in Hollywood.
>
> All of our printing was being done at the Hollywood office so all the branch offices in the East were dependent upon us for all of the tests to ship out. We realized that we had to get as many tests shipped to the branch offices as possible and had to do it that very day if we were going to stay in business. We knew once a picket line was placed around our offices we would have difficulty shipping materials. That afternoon our entire office force went into the warehouse where we packed all of the tests on hand, placed the boxes on wooden skids and loaded all of the materials that we possibly could on huge freight trucks. We

shipped them to our Madison and New Cumberland offices. We were amazed how many tons of tests we were able to get out of the warehouse in one afternoon.

Ethel was incensed over the union's charge of unfair labor practices. As one benefit, she gave each employee his/her birthday off with pay. It started out to be restricted to just the actual birth date, but after a while that was relaxed, and the employee could take off any day during the year as long it did not create some conflict with work schedules. It turned out that under the labor law any such time off had to be taken within the given week of the birthday, so she was in violation in that sense, although it certainly was a loss to the employees to no longer have a choice of dates. Ethel went on about the picket line:

> As expected, the next morning, there were pickets walking the sidewalk in front of the building. The Union also placed more pickets in our parking lot adjacent to the warehouse. They were the roughest looking bunch of men I have ever seen. The pickets began threatening us as we drove through their line into the parking lot. Union officials phoned the homes of a number of our employees and threatened them if they were to try to come to work. Since we had several European refugees working for us who had language difficulties it was particularly hard on them since they could not understand what was going on.
>
> We called the Los Angeles office of the Merchants and Manufacturers Association (an employers' rights advocacy group). I shall always be indebted to this group for the fine advice and help they gave us during this trying period. They were most helpful in telling us just what we could say to the employees and what we could not.
>
> Now when there was a union picket line around a company no truck driver who belonged to the Teamsters Union was allowed to cross that picket line. You could see what this did to us as far as trying to ship any of the booklets that we were trying to print inside. It was almost impossible to get freight out of our building. We learned through the Merchants and Manufacturers Association of the trucking

company, I think it was called the G. I. Trucking Company that had a court injunction that forbade unions from stopping them when they tried to cross a picket line. This is another company I shall always be grateful to because the G. I. Trucking Company really saved CTB's life in that they would send their trucks into our warehouse, take the printed tests and boxes out and deposit them on the freight docks in another part of town. They would put them on the freight docks of the national trucking companies and in that way we were able to continue shipping tests. It sounds very simple now but it did involve a lot of difficulties since many times the pickets would attempt to throw lighted cigarettes into the truckloads of tests as they went out or do anything possible to thwart our attempt to get them shipped. We found it necessary to keep armed guards around our building at nearly $2,000 per month to prevent the building from being set on fire. Many were the evenings that Bill Melton and Bob Olloman had to literally smuggle tests out of the building and take them out to the Burbank airport in order to get them shipped airfreight to one of our branches in time to meet a customer's needs.

The union pickets caused other problems, too, by not allowing trash trucks to come in and pick up the trash in the plant. A tremendous amount of waste paper accumulates in one 24-hour period at a printing plant. Since the union prevented trash truck drivers from coming through the lines the paper piled up in the print shop. The bindery and print shop employees tried to help by bringing in empty sacks and bags each morning, filling them with trash paper and taking them home each night, facing the jeers and bad calling by the pickets.

We had been having fire inspections about once a year, but suddenly fire inspectors began showing up at the plant almost every day to see what the situation was. The coincidence of having union troubles and suddenly having frequent fire inspections was too great for us to accept as being pure chance (part of the Los Angeles Fire Department was AFL Union). The fire inspectors kept telling us that we had to get the trash out of the building. The pickets kept telling us they would not allow trash trucks to cross their picket line. Of course all they were doing was bringing pressure to bear on us to sign the agreement with the union so that the picket line would be removed and the trash trucks could come in. I was determined that I would not be pressured into signing any such agreement.

It finally got to the point that a warrant was issued for my arrest charging me with aiding and abetting a fire hazard. When I went to court I pleaded not guilty and demanded a jury trial. With my father's help [Ethel's father was a former police officer who became a detective lieutenant] the charges were finally dismissed. This just gives some indication, however, as to how far unions do go in trying to force their demands.

The picketing went on from September until the following June or July without interruption. The pickets were there every day. They made the same threats and nuisance of themselves day after day. We finally got so that we felt that they were almost a part of the organization and we came to take them for granted and came to accept the handicaps under which we were operating as a matter of fact.

We all went on vacation in July, and at that time, if I remember correctly, we closed down the offices and everyone went on vacation at the same time. We were able to do that then. When we came back from our vacations, the pickets were gone. They had held out and made a nuisance of themselves for eleven months but we had won the battle, as they did not return. The employees who never wanted to join a union did not have to do so, and they continued with us as trusted employees.

Later, Ethel continued about printing the test materials:

Now I have to go back here a little ways and say that for several years prior to that time we had realized it was not too efficient for us to be shipping paper from eastern Canada to

59

California, printing it and then shipping two thirds of our test booklets or printed materials to our branch offices. We had for years before we contacted George Banta and his large printing company in Wisconsin to see if they would be able someday to help us with our printing. The George Banta Company had for years been known as probably the biggest printer of school workbooks and things of that nature. So we had been thinking for a long time of someday having our printing done in the Midwest where it would be closer to the supply of paper. We had also noticed through the years that it complicated our operations by trying to have two different types of personnel: print shop personnel and office personnel. We had also been feeling the pinch more and more in the 60-year-old building in that the printing equipment in the back took up so much room that could have been used for stocking our warehouse. The 1950 edition of the *California Achievement Test* had come out and with all the levels and forms of the test we had a need for a great deal more inventory and therefore more warehouse space. Well, the pickets were gone and we could then sit down and decide just what we were going to do about this printing operation. We decided that we would arrange with the George Banta Company in Wisconsin to do all the printing of our test booklets and accessory items in the future. So by 1952 we proceeded to sell our printing presses and all of our bindery equipment and utilize the space for warehousing.

Ethel's parents dressed her as a newsboy and in other boys' outfits.

Ethel in high school.

Ethel with her parents and brother Richard.

Ethel and Willis betrothed.

The fateful bear hunting excursion.
Willis at left.

Willis at left, O'Brien right.

The Hollywood Hills home.

Ethel's brother, Richard, third from the right.
Janice front left.

Hollywood Boulevard shipping and receiving.

California Test Bureau Hollywood Boulevard staff.

Ernest W. Tiegs, co-author with
Willis Clark

Elizabeth T. Sullivan, co-author of
California Test of Mental Maturity

Warren Hook, CTB executive,
family friend, constant companion

George Gracey, Eastern Region
Branch Manager

Harry Wardenberg, CTB
Financial Vice-President

The first four CTB educational consultants: Robert Dion, NH;
Marlin Schrader, KS; John Hughes, PA; John Armstrong, WI

In 1938 IBM introduced
its revolutionary 805 Test
Scoring Machine.

Dr. Shanner and the author
examine the new IBM equipment.

The Scoring Department.

A CTB exhibit booth.

CTB in Pennsylvania.

Warehousing required expert management.

Employees participated in "Clark's Follies."
The author hams it up on stage with a colleague.

Ethel and June with Ethel's parents on their 50th
wedding anniversary.

Ethel, Warren, and Willis are honored on a CTB anniversary.

Ethel had a new building constructed for CTB's move to Monterey.

A meeting with CTB consultants at Pebble Beach, California.

Ethel Clark in her Monterey office overlooking the airport in the early 1960s.

The new Monterey facility was very upscale.

Author and husband Frank Duran.

Children Patricia, Timothy Duran.

Willis and Ethel both in hospital.

Financial Advisors T. E. O'Sullivan
and Paul Lee met with Ethel to
arrange CTB sale to McGraw-Hill.

The CTB/McGraw-Hill Executive Committee in the 1970s:
Dave Deffley, Frank Snyder, William Satchell, Ed Reilly, and
John Martin with the author.

McGraw-Hill Takes Over Cal Test Bureau

The California Test Bureau of Monterey yesterday became a wholly owned subsidiary of McGraw-Hill, Inc., one of the largest U.S. book publishing houses.

Edward E. Booher, new chairman of the board of CTB; Robert W. Locke, new president of CTB and John Cooke, vice president and general counsel of McGraw-Hill, held a series of meetings at the plant at Del Monte Research Park to launch the new operation.

As executive vice president and general manager of CTB, Francis S. Fox will be the chief operating officer and is due to move here Sept. 2 from New York. He has purchased a home in Carmel Valley and will soon be joined by his wife, Norma, and their daughters, ages 10 and 14.

Mrs. Ethel Clark, who resigned as president and chairman of the board of California Test Bureau, is being retained as a consultant, it was announced by Donald C. McGraw, president of the publishing company.

Mrs. June Duran, will remain as administrative vice president and Maurice Wilson as secretary-treasurer.

Cal Test will remain a corporate entity for the balance of the year, but may then be absorbed by the parent company, it was stated. Its acquisition will enable McGraw-Hill, as leading publisher of school textbooks, to round out its school service operation, it; was explained. The growth of the market for standardized tests is expected to increase by 25 per cent during each of the next 5 years, forecasting a considerable expansion of the Monterey subsidiary. For the time being, there will be no change in its operation, McGraw-Hill officials said.

Monterey Peninsula Herald
Friday, August 27, 1965.   10

McGraw-Hill CEO Harold W. McGraw Jr. holds the shovel with the author during the groundbreaking in 1974 for CTB/McGraw-Hill's second Monterey location, on Garden Road.

Author June Duran Stock speaks at CTB/McGraw-Hill's 85th anniversary celebration at company headquarters in Monterey in 2011.
The pictorial timeline of CTB begins with Ethel's photograph at far left.

The author, second from left, is honored during the event by daughter Patricia Duran, left; Tom Torlakson, California State Superintendent of Public Instruction; John Covington, Superintendent of the Kansas City, Missouri School District (the first district to respond to Ethel's 25-cent gamble); son Timothy Duran; and CTB President Ellen Haley.
Photos this page: William Roden/New Dawn Studios

CHAPTER 12

FRANK

I first met Frank Duran at a pre-party cocktail hour at our home in 1939 and later became more acquainted with him at a Halloween party at the Jonathan Club in Los Angeles. Among the guests at the cocktail party was my friend, Kate Kirchner, who had brought along her friend, Frank Duran. Ethel, Willis, and Warren along with a handful of assorted guests joined us. When the group set out for the Jonathan Club, a trip from Hollywood to downtown Los Angeles, Frank was the driver in a beat-up second hand car with Kate and two other couples. As the two cars were following close together, it was easy to see that Frank was weaving in and out of traffic and driving pretty fast. Darn if he wasn't stopped and given a ticket that threw me into despair because I thought that would ruin the party for Frank and Kate. When Frank didn't seem at all distressed, I thanked him for being such a good sport, and he answered, "Oh, don't worry, I'm used to that."

The next day Frank called me for a date, but I wouldn't accept until I cleared it with Kate. Kate gave her blessing to the situation, indicating Frank was just a casual friend. That was the start of the romance. One thing that did seem unusual to me was that Frank always brought me home early from our dates, which I interpreted as his way of caring for my health and being sure I got a good night's sleep. It wasn't until after we were married that I learned that after dropping me off, he would go home so he could "figure the races."

There was about 12 years difference in our ages, which didn't become a problem until much later on. Also, perhaps because Frank was much older than I, Ethel seemed at first to take a special interest in him and approve of him as a potential family member. He was a very congenial, friendly sort of guy with an easy smile and was very nice looking in a manly way. At one time he had trained to be a boxer but gave it up when he was really badly beaten up in the ring. He had come down from Canada to be with his father, who had left the family a couple of years earlier. Frank found life in Canada very boring with almost no future, and his father's adventuresome nature seemed to repeat itself in Frank. He was at loose ends for a while, living in a boarding house and, at times, was in with sort of a bad crowd. An older man spotted Frank as someone who badly needed guidance and arranged for Frank to go to a trade school in Los Angeles. There he learned welding and body and fender work, and he easily got a job as a service manager for a Pontiac agency. That's when he met me.

I completed three years of college before I got married, but it became apparent that if I were to continue with a career at CTB I would need to further my education. I had skipped a grade in grammar school and did well in high school, graduating at the age of fifteen. I wanted to become a famous medical research doctor. Willis went with me when I enrolled at the University of California, Los Angeles. I remember the counselor warned us that taking the full 16 credit hours per semester was a heavy load. Willis brushed the warning aside, however, and had me sign up for 18 units. I almost suffered a collapse from trying to keep up with the work. This coincided with my parents' rigid views about earning one's keep. Their views translated into a very big burden for me. Going to UCLA from where we lived required four bus transfers each way. I was also doing the housework, including washing the dishes, making the beds, and straightening up the house. My parents had a wretched habit of throwing newspapers on the floor after reading them in bed in the morning. It made me gnash my teeth picking up after them while still having to do my homework, with Willis always pressuring me to do better.

I stopped college for a while and went to secretarial school. The skills I learned there helped me at CTB. After I was married, I went back to school nights at USC and earned a B.A. degree. I went on to earn a school psychometrist credential. A psychometrist was responsible for the administration and scoring of psychological and neuropsychological tests under the supervision of a clinical psychologist or clinical neuropsychologist. A psychometrist also made note of behavioral observations during the course of the assessment, which could be used in the interpretation of the test results. Naturally this was invaluable information at CTB. (Still later I went to law school and by the time McGraw-Hill purchased CTB in 1965, my work towards a law degree put me in good standing with corporate personnel at McGraw-Hill. I received my law degree in 1978.)

A marriage date for Frank and me was set for April 26, 1940, although it originally was planned for May. One of the employees at the schoolbook depository began spreading the rumor that we had to move the marriage date because I was pregnant. The word got back to Ethel. This particular employee was one Ethel disliked and to even write about this phase of the June-Frank "courtship" is sickening. Ethel had a way of using that strong, demanding personality of hers to get things her way, sometimes insidiously, and this was one of those times. She started in on Frank. Knowing that he had been a boxer, she began asking how he could tolerate what was being said about me and finished with the taunt that if he were a real man, he would do something about it. She really laid it on him and tried to shame him in front of me because he wasn't avenging my honor. One evening she arranged for Frank, Willis, Warren, and herself to be at the depository when the fellow spreading the rumor was there. Ethel pointed him out to Frank and asked Frank what he was going to do about it, saying he ought to beat him up and similar inflammatory remarks. Well, Frank felt he had to do something, so he socked the fellow, knocking out a couple of teeth. It was so awful because the fellow didn't know what was happening to him and certainly was in no shape to fight back. Naturally the fellow left and Ethel got her way, enjoying every moment of it. Frank felt used, Willis said nothing, Warren disappeared, and I was aghast when I heard about it. The total irony was that although Ethel certainly started the whole thing, she later accused Frank of brutality and other unsavory conduct—and that's the way it would be between Ethel and Frank.

The original plan was for a church wedding. However, as the guest list increased and the costs went up, it seemed a lot more logical to go to Las Vegas for the event. When the time drew closer, Ethel became more and more unpleasant to Frank, and the ride to Las Vegas was extremely tense. She didn't speak a word the whole time. The wedding itself was very brief, and, to round out the scene, the pastor was drunk and married us under the wrong name. Warren had arranged for a photographer to take the wedding pictures, but the photos were so bad that we never even ordered a copy. Everyone was staring straight ahead, no smiles or warmth. It had all the appearances of a shotgun wedding.

After the wedding, everyone headed in different directions to the gaming tables. I trotted along after Frank, who headed for the craps table. The Clarks and Warren settled in at roulette. There was nothing in the way of a wedding dinner, and everyone was so involved with the gambling that I finally went back to our room. So much for the romantic desert night, with the sand kissing the moonlit sky. It was even more disturbing to discover that Warren had been assigned mysteriously to the room next door.

Before the wedding date, I had started looking for an apartment. Meanwhile Ethel and Willis were planning to go ahead with building their new home. Both Frank and I wanted to get away from the Clarks, but it was hard to rebut the Clarks' stance that the Durans could live cheaper in the new house than in an apartment. Ethel claimed that the new house would never have been planned if they knew I was going to get married, and she inaugurated accusations against me for putting the Clarks in this position. As Warren was paying for his square footage in the new house, the same terms would apply to Frank and me, and we would all live happily together.

As for me being married, there was no question that Ethel had a hard time "losing" me, so she put plenty of barricades along the way. One concern was that Frank was going to impregnate me right away. I think that's why she put Warren in the room next to us on our wedding night—she probably had him listening in on us. That would have been typical strategy for Ethel. She put up obstacles to us finding an apartment away from home and kept insisting it would be so much cheaper for us to stay with her (under her control). The rent she charged would be a fraction of what we would pay elsewhere. She took an "it's going to be this way or else" stance. Sad to say, we gave in.

Although America was at war, the Clarks somehow were able to get enough materials to build their beautiful home in the Hollywood Hills at the corner of Mulholland and Outpost, very near the famous Hollywood sign. On a clear day they had a fabulous view of greater Los Angeles, all the way down to the ocean.

When the house on Alta Vista was sold in 1941, all five parties moved into the new house.

CHAPTER 13

"JUST CONSIDER THE SOURCE"

Ethel loved to give parties, and oh the parties she gave when the family moved to Mulholland Drive with its magnificent view of the city! Of the many she gave, two in particular were standouts. One was a Western-themed event with costumes, a jail constructed on the spot, and a huge barbecue that was catered and included all the fixings of an Old West "on the trail" chuck-wagon dinner. Willis wore an authentic outfit with a green visor and garters to hold up his sleeves so they wouldn't get soiled. Warren was the sheriff, with a silver star on his shirt and jail keys dangling from his belt. Ethel was a madam wearing a dress with a short skirt, net stockings, a boa, and a large feathered hat. The dress and stockings were bright red, and the red hat had an elongated black feather. She loved the role and jumped into it. Signs were printed to denote locations such as Myrna's Hole for the bar (Myrna was one of Ethel's nicknames), Erasmus B. Black as Judge, the jail, and the hotel. One sign even pointed to boot hill, which led to the bathrooms. Some of the guests were bused from Long Beach so there wouldn't be a problem with having to drive home after some serious drinking at the saloon. Warren, as sheriff, arrested many of the guests for a variety of indiscretions and placed them in the jail, where they had to chugalug a stein of beer to get released. It was a memorable evening spoken about for weeks after the party.

Perhaps the topper of all the parties was a luau everyone attended in costume. There was no stopping Ethel in making the arrangements. She had the caterers bring a boar (kulua pig) and finish slow-cooking it in a shallow pit that was dug in the yard. There were platters of Hawaiian food, including banana coconut guava cake, beef teriyaki, char siu (delicious rich red spareribs), chicken luau (chicken cooked with taro leaves and coconut), fried rice, and haupia (a traditional, coconut-flavored Hawaiian dessert). The food circled a big fountain with a block of ice in the center and a rum punch concoction poured over it. The theory was that the melting ice would continually dilute the rum punch so the guests would not get drunk. That was the concept anyway. However, the caterers didn't know the crowd they were dealing with. There were cups for the guests to ladle out the drinks themselves. The drinks went down easily and so did the rum in the fountain. The rum was constantly refilled because the ice didn't melt fast enough to provide enough liquid for the drinks, and after a while it didn't much matter.

As the evening wore on, the guests participated in Hawaiian dances accompanied by authentic music of the Islands. The more rum consumed, the more "authentic" and creative the interpretations of the dances became. The caterers hadn't allowed enough time for the boar to be completely roasted, so dinner was served late, well after the guests had become "roasted." Those who were still standing managed to eat something. It seemed that the crowd had thinned out, but that was only because so many people had passed out. Frank was found asleep, tucked away contentedly under a hibiscus bush. He could not be roused. Neither could many of the others who were in the same shape.

*   *   *

Willis, Ethel, and I, with Warren driving, all went to work together while Frank commuted to Cal Ship in San Pedro, a round trip of about 70 miles. He was a welding supervisor, giving him exemption from military duty, which was a sore point with Ethel. The stigma of young men not being in the service grew stronger as war fever grew. Ethel, who eagerly wanted her new son-in-law to join the ranks, was very vocal about her feelings. She often expressed these feelings at breakfast, which got the day off to a miserable start. It didn't matter to her that Frank, who was a skilled welder (a trade much in demand at the time), had been hired as an instructor where the Liberty ships were being built, and had won several awards for his inventions there. She wanted him in uniform! Now! The situation was exacerbated because Ethel had told all her friends that Frank would be one of the first to enlist, but he hadn't enlisted. At one time Frank told her, "Ethel, you sure would make a good recruiting officer." People did not speak to Ethel that way, so the line was drawn and was not to be erased. The antagonism grew until Willis eventually stepped in to turn down the volume.

Another factor that could be plugged into the Ethel versus Frank hostility was Frank's distaste of the Ethel/Warren situation based on his observations at home. Also, years later he told me that shortly after we were married Ethel "came on" to him, and he disgustedly turned her down. Well, no woman wants to be slighted, but really! No wonder Frank spent so much time away from "home."

Frank was originally assigned to the graveyard shift, and the adjustment to those difficult hours was a real problem for both of us. Working such disparate hours gave us very little time together, but we were happy that Frank did not have to go into the service. The problems with getting food using ration stamps, using blackout curtains, and the pressure to donate cooking pots and pans to be melted down for use as ammunition were no different for us than for most other people in Los Angeles and elsewhere. However, the long drive and irregular hours took their toll on Frank, who had a terrible time trying to sleep in the daytime.

Frank didn't need to sleep all the time; eventually nature took its course, and I became pregnant in 1942. At first Ethel had a difficult time accepting that she would become a grandmother but eventually became involved in the process. Because we were living on a hillside in a rather remote area, she worried that we would not have time to get me to a hospital. She decided to take matters into her own hands. She arranged to have a gas tank delivered and installed in the side of the hill flanking the house. She even had it filled with gas despite all the rationing restrictions. As far as I know the tank is still there, perhaps further down the hill than it was originally. As it turned out, Frank was able to get me to the hospital on time. Tim was born in 1943. We had a rather large bedroom, so turning it into a combination bedroom/ nursery was not too much of a problem; however, coping with the varying hours of Frank's job was a problem. Frank finally was able to get regular working hours, and we were able to establish some sort of normalcy.

There were difficult times with the Ethel/Warren situation. Frank found it increasingly distasteful and also often referred to Ethel's "rejection" of him after the awkward situation where she "came on" to him. Right from the beginning Frank had a dislike for Ethel and Warren, individually and collectively. I wasn't aware of the depth of his feelings until quite a while into our marriage. Ethel's "hitting on" him was distasteful enough, but he bristled at the nightly foot rubs with Ethel in Warren's lap. This all took place while we were in my parents' Hollywood Hills house, where Ethel and Willis had one wing on the top floor. Frank and I had the other wing, with Warren's room between the two wings.

Frank confided in me that one day he came home unexpectedly to see Warren running out of Ethel's bedroom tucking in his shirt. Naturally he concluded that it was verification of what he suspected had been going on the entire time. Frank went so far as to tell me that he believed Ethel was a slut. It was difficult to have that articulated; nonetheless, there was little I could do to dispute his feelings about my mother. Frank was among many who couldn't understand why Willis never took any action.

Looking back now, I think I know why, but who can say for sure. Willis was the ultimate scholar you see. He loved academics, and he particularly loved creating tests and developing the case history approach. He wrote scads of bulletins and articles on testing and related subjects. With Warren around to be at Ethel's beck and call, Willis was freed from all the nuisance details of daily living with her. Perhaps this included sexual demands as well. If challenged about any of Warren's deeds, Willis would use one of his favorite expressions, "Well, just consider the source," ending the conversation. I did take the gossip about Ethel and Warren to him. He dismissed me with a casual wave of the hand. That was the end of that. I came to realize that my father did not take a hard stance against Warren's entrenchment into the marriage and Ethel's reliance on him. This gave my father his own privacy instead of having to do chores and put up with Ethel's whims.

Despite all of this, there was the unending camaraderie among the three of them, which included pre-dinner drinks and games of rummy that they played for money. The game was one of the offshoots of basic rummy. They called it racehorse rummy. Usually, after an hour of the game, Warren or Ethel would fix dinner, begrudging the time away from the game. Score was kept and they would settle up at the end of the month. I remember that Warren seemed to be the heavy winner. This irritated Ethel, who accused him of cheating. The drink of choice was Ballantine's scotch taken with a little ice and water. They went through a fifth every evening.

At long last, after five years of living in such a tense situation, an opportunity arose to purchase a little cabin in the Hollywood Hills, and Frank and I were able to buy it and move. Looking back, this was a very fortuitous action; for $2500 we were able to get two and one-half oak-covered acres overlooking the San Fernando Valley, along with the cabin that was tossed in as uninhabitable. The cabin had once belonged to John Ford, a movie director, and was very rustic indeed. It consisted of a long living room, a brick fireplace, a covered deck, a Murphy's bed, a kitchen, and a modified bathroom that hung over a cesspool. With the trees and the beautiful view, who could ask for anything more—certainly not the squirrels, other wildlife, and invasive plants that also called it home.

Frank was good with his hands and had experience with home improvement, having worked at his father's very old apartment house in downtown Los Angeles. He knew enough about electricity, painting, and carpentry to put the cabin back together again into reasonably good condition. A closet off the living room became a bedroom for Tim. The cesspool became a septic tank, and the covered deck another bedroom/sunroom. Altogether, we lived there eleven years and during that time our daughter, Patricia, was born.

During those eleven years we planned to build a "regular" house on the hillside above the cabin and eventually built one in 1955. The architect did a wonderful job fitting the new home into the contours of the hills, and a beautiful split-level home came into being.

Before building, I had met with Ethel and Willis asking for assurance that their very tentative plans to move CTB to a larger space would not mean leaving the Los Angeles area, and I was told that would never happen. So after we had moved into our new home and been there about six months, Ethel announced that she was going to move the company to Monterey. We were devastated. Frank had recently leased property in Culver City across from MGM studios, where he was developing quite a clientele for his body and fender work. I was tied to CTB in many ways.

CHAPTER 14

SHANNER

The war had given quite an impetus to testing, and sales of Willis's tests grew. Along with that came increasing inquiries from customers about the proper use of tests, "norming," and other technical questions that the remaining staff were not qualified to answer. The scoring service was also beginning to pick up, so Ethel's little testing business obviously was going to need more professional attention.

Ethel had never involved herself in the intricacies of test development and, in fact, found it very boring, but who was going to do it? There were only one or two people on the staff who had real testing experience. One of those was Bishop Estes, a bubbly older fellow who raced about quoting "No rest for the wicked and the righteous don't have time to rest" or "Trifles make perfection, but perfection is no trifle." Perhaps they were words to live by, but they became very tiresome after a while. We were all working very hard to keep the company alive and really didn't need goading, not that he really meant it that way. Bishop, like the rest of us, was performing three or four jobs each day, ranging from stocking the shelves to taking orders, packing shipments, and, in his case, answering customer inquiries; however, his knowledge only extended so far, and more substantive answers were required.

The obvious answer was Willis, who by now was spending so much time in the evening and weekends dealing with CTB's customer correspondence, in addition to completing his doctoral dissertation and still serving as Director of Research at Los Angeles County Schools. Willis was torn with loyalties and worn out by his many obligations. In 1941, Willis received his Ed.D. from USC. Reluctantly he finally decided to resign from the County; in 1944 Willis made the break and joined Ethel at CTB.

After Willis joined CTB, Ethel added some private offices, a sort of his and hers arrangement next to each other with a very strange wallpaper background above the wainscoting, showing a scene of Old London. Later, when he joined CTB, Dr. Tiegs was put in an office close to Willis, and I was put next to an entry door where I could serve as the intake person, attend to personnel matters, and conduct testing for individuals going to the newly operational Educational and Vocational Guidance Clinic, which was Willis's idea. The slowly growing test research and development offices were positioned next to the Hollywood Boulevard window, which did not allow much privacy but was great for looking out as well as looking in.

In addition to starting the Clinic, Willis became interested in developing a test for the selection of nurses, a jump into otherwise uncharted waters. The Los Angeles General Hospital's School of Nursing was instrumental in helping advance this new approach. Another new endeavor was related to industrial uses of tests, primarily for employee selection. Willis decided to set up a department within the company, calling it Industrial Psychological Services, with a very dynamic director, Dr. Joice Stone.

Willis had looked up to Ernest Tiegs as his mentor and collaborator, and there was no doubt of Tiegs's fondness for Willis. Their discussions of statistics and testing and variations on the theme went on for many, many years. The demands on Willis piled up, the company grew along with the need for more sophisticated responses to customer inquiries, and there was increased motivation to develop even more tests. So it was decided that Tiegs would leave the University of Southern California and team up with Willis. On paper this seemed like a good idea, but in reality it led to slight clashes of strong personalities.

Tiegs had problems with the air conditioning in his new office. He never seemed to be able to get it adjusted properly. So Tiegs, who was quite bald, began wearing a rather colorful, plaid tam-o'-shanter with a tassel on top to protect his head. It made quite a picture as people walking by his office on Hollywood Boulevard could look in at Tiegs at work, tam-o'-shanter and all. Tiegs also liked to smoke. He smoked big, powerful cigars. One of the things that got ignored in the early negotiations for Tiegs' new job was that Ethel was adamant about not being around smokers, and, in fact, there was no smoking allowed at CTB at all except in a small area close to the back entrance. Ethel's direct order on this had not affected Tiegs whatsoever. He liked to smoke and he was going to smoke—too bad about Ethel. Things really came to a head because a lot of other employees also liked to smoke and resented being relegated to a little area while Tiegs was free to smoke in his office. Still, things went along pretty well until one train trip to Chicago.

Airplane travel was not customary in those days, and Chicago was a long train ride from Los Angeles. It was the long-standing custom for Ethel, Willis, and Warren to have a gin rummy game before dinner every night. Tiegs was invited to join, but that meant his cigar came along with him. It didn't take very long for the compartment's small space to fill up with polluted air. Ethel was truly affected by cigarette smoke and even more so by cigar smoke. She showed her displeasure by putting on the performance of a victim that was worthy of an Academy Award. She made disparaging comments, coughed as if she were Sarah Bernhardt dying of consumption as *Camille*, and showed other indications of displeasure. Tiegs ignored her performances and never made any attempt to stop smoking. We all went through one day of this, and Ethel, as was her usual MO, did not confront Tiegs herself but went through Willis to complain. Willis did not like any kind of confrontation but did mention the smoking to Tiegs. It didn't work. By the time we got to Chicago, a small war was brewing, and we still had to make the return trip home. Speaking of brewing, it was customary for everyone to have cocktails along with the gin rummy games, but Tiegs did not drink anything but beer, much to Ethel's annoyance. Somehow we got through the train trip; however, things were never quite the same again. It led to obvious hostility between Ethel and Tiegs, with neither one of them willing to give in on anything, and Willis being batted back and forth between them like a tennis ball.

About this time a possible move to Monterey was being considered. Tiegs let it be known there was no way he would move to wherever the new building would be located. This was fine with Ethel.

*   *   *

Ethel was always interested in various kinds of promotional efforts and advertising, so when the Addressograph machine came to her attention, she was sure there would be applications at CTB. The Addressograph machine itself was like a cross between a linotype and a typewriter. It stamped out label-sized steel plates that had a series of slots along the top. The slots could be used for any number of identification purposes. In this case, it was used to key which customers used what tests and that information was then punched into the steel plates and inserted into card-sized frames to be used in promotional efforts. The Addressograph label could be notched so that it could be used for many different kinds of identification. That information could then be sorted out by test product and followed up with information about a related test. For example, the *California Achievement Test* customers could be sorted out, and then information about the *California Test of Mental Maturity* could be sent to those customers. These procedures all seem very rudimentary compared with today's mass mailings, but this was a start and was very useful. At one time Willis became interested in preparing customer questionnaires for each test, in which he highlighted the features of each of the products and indicated how they were all interrelated. The idea was to disperse the questionnaires to possible customers by including copies in shipments to them. It turned out to be a very good sales tool.

An incident in connection with an advertising brochure tied in with our mailing list brought home how important a good proofreader is to the printing/publishing business. We were launching a new product called *Test of English Usage*. The brochure was designed, printed, and sent to our entire mailing list via Addressograph. In just a few days we were inundated with everything from humorous to downright painfully humiliating comments from customers. Remember, this was a test of English USAGE! The copy read "To *Whoever* It May Concern" and went on to explain that this instrument tested English "gram*mer!*"

I remember quite distinctly an applicant for Addressograph operator who made quite an impression. She was a very young, very thin, very emaciated person who looked as though a big gust of wind would blow her away. Somehow the interview wound its way around to her home situation and her particular interest in working nights on the job. Upon further inquiry it turned out that the reason she wanted to keep those hours was because her mother used their home on certain nights so she could "roll sailors," a job title with which I was unfamiliar. I saved myself embarrassment by not asking the applicant what it meant, but found out later, after hiring her. As it turned out, she was a very good worker.

Ethel had been after Willis to change the appearance of his test booklets for years. She said, "Willis, those test booklets with all those charts and graphs are enough to shock the teachers and scare the hell out of the kids taking tests." Over Willis's protest, in about 1955 she retained the Raymond Lowry Company to revamp the appearance of the tests and accompanying materials and to make any other changes they felt would enhance CTB's image. Their evaluation of the testing materials resulted in the introduction of "Eye-Ease" paper that had a soft, light-greenish tint that was considered ophthalmologically correct, with almost everything printed in dark green ink. Envelopes and letterheads were embossed, and a logo was developed of a big C with a check mark inside. It was extremely effective. They also designed tie clips with the logo for the consultants to wear, but they hated them and didn't wear them except when Ethel was around. There was a popular song at the time, "Green Eyes," from which several in-house parodies were produced in conjunction with our new look. I remember one that went something like "All tests are green now/They have that Lowry scheme now/We're strictly on the beam now/As anyone can see." Bandleader Jimmy Dorsey and vocalists Helen O'Connell and Bob Eberly, who had the most popular recording of the song, didn't need to feel threatened by our rendition. The place was abuzz with all this and the retention of the Lowry Company to revamp the appearance of the tests and accompanying materials.

There is no question that the most important center of activity had to do with test development itself. The company had acquired sufficient prestige to attract professional interest in the quality of the research going on, and several new tests were planned and measurement specialists were hired. Dr. William Shanner, who was especially versed in statistical problems relating to tests and measurement, joined the staff in about 1954. Dr. Shanner came to CTB from the University of Oklahoma and immediately filled a void with his excellent background in educational statistics, his creative thinking, and his all-around good nature. He and Ethel got along well because he liked to drink and tell stories, and Willis was overjoyed to find a professional who cared about academic achievement and helping individuals meet their full potential. He had many other assets, among them a great interest in chemistry; in fact, he invented a chemical treatment for cantaloupes that retards mold and spoilage and that is still in use today. His role in the company and particularly his rapport with the Clarks made him the object of some jealousy on the part of some of the other professionals. He would often drop by the Clarks' home after work and have a drink, and they looked forward to seeing him.

He and Willis worked together closely and became almost inseparable. Shanner, as he was called, consulted for hours and hours with Willis in developing the proper approach to a new standardization of the newly revised *California Achievement Test* and *California Test of Mental Maturity,* known as a dual standardization. This was done with the ultimate goal of establishing an accurate prediction of a student's anticipated achievement.

Shanner had an inordinate capacity for whiskey. In one night he could drink a whole fifth of bourbon and not show any effects from it. One evening he was pulled over by the California Highway Patrol for drunk driving and booked for that offense. His case eventually came up for trial, and he insisted on a jury trial. Shanner wasn't disturbed by any of this. His knowledge of statistics and human nature worked to his advantage. The judge was upset with him as he began to build his case on his physical strength, his capacity for drinking, and his conditioning for the same. He drew on statistical information to show that with his background and capacity he couldn't possibly be drunk, but Shanner wasn't exhibiting his superior knowledge to impress the judge. His showmanship was directed towards a very attractive lady on the jury. He had told his attorney that he only needed one jury member to side with him. Sure enough, the lady declared him "not guilty," and he got off because of a hung jury.

Nonetheless, despite his charm and knowledge, Shanner's drinking began to be a problem. After the move to Monterey, the neighboring airport bar began to be his office, and he could often be found there discussing world affairs or espousing on any variety of subjects. Since he was the company's authority on norming and statistical applications to test results, his absences began to cause some real problems. Still, it was almost impossible to be angry with him.

He developed a bad habit of agreeing to answer very technical questions received in correspondence, then putting them aside, and, at times, even denying he had any awareness of them being assigned to him. The company developed a system to track letters, logging them in when they were assigned to the appropriate personnel and logging them out when they were answered. It became obvious that Shanner wasn't acknowledging the letters, let alone answering them. Things eventually got to the point that he had to either do his job or be let go. That would hurt the company, but something had to be done. He was so believable when he would explain his absences or nonperformance, and he was so brilliant. Willis, in particular, was devastated by the turn of events for he looked upon Shanner as his son. And Ethel felt the loss of such a good companion. He was eventually let go; after he left, someone went through his desk and found wads of letters from key customers or educational leaders that had never been touched. Despite his forced resignation, following Willis's death in 1964, Shanner arranged to have a special cabinet made to display some of Willis's works and favorite references and then pulled together a memorial ceremony in his honor. The cabinet still stands in the CTB/McGraw-Hill building.

Willis went full bore on completing his tests for individual case history purposes. In addition to the *California Achievement Test* and the *California Test of Mental Maturity*, other tests he created, usually with at least one other recognized authority, were:

California Test of Personality
Vocational Interest Analysis
Personnel Selection and Classification Test
California Capacity Questionnaire
Lee-Clark Arithmetic Fundamentals Survey Test
Mental Health Analysis
Pre-Tests of Vision, Hearing and Motor Coordination
Lee-Clark Reading Readiness Series

In addition to his efforts to have the equivalent of a quantified case history for each student, Willis had a similar passion for ensuring that test results were used properly. He wrote a number of Educational Bulletins "with the belief that results obtained with evaluation instruments should be used to improve instruction and guidance and counseling."

The titles themselves reflect his earnest attempts to promote this belief, and, at his insistence, they were free.

Educational Bulletins
No. 1. *How Tests Can Improve Your Schools*
No. 2. *How to Select Tests*
No. 3. *How to Conduct A Survey*
No. 4. *Administrative Uses of Test Results*
No. 5. *Teacher Uses of Test Results*
No. 6. *A Suggested Testing Program for Educational Diagnosis and Pupil Guidance*
No. 7. *Conducting High School Guidance Programs*
No. 8. *Planning the Elementary School Testing Program*
No. 9. *Identifying Difficulties in Learning Arithmetic*
No. 10. *Diagnosis in the Reading Program*
No. 11. *Appraising Personality and Social Adjustment*
No. 12. *Use of Tests and Inventories in Vocational Guidance and Rehabilitation*
No. 13. *Use of Standardized Tests in Correctional Institutions*
No. 14. *The Proper Use of Intelligence Tests*
No. 15. *Vocational Guidance for Junior and Senior High School Pupils*
No. 16. *Guiding Child and Adolescent Development in the Modern School*
No. 17. *Techniques of Follow-up Study of School-Leavers*
No. 18. *Educational Diagnosis*
No. 19. *Improving Educational Opportunities Through an Adequate Guidance Program*
No. 20. *Articulated and Integrated Measuring Instruments for Practical Evaluation Programs*
No. 21. *Guidance Testing and the Identification of Pupil Characteristics*
No. 22. *Using Test Results to Identify Student Needs for Corrective Instruction*
No. 23. *Using Tape-Recorded Instructions to Administer Standardized Tests*

With interest increasing in CTB, its philosophy, and professional personnel, other authors became interested in being published. The catalog expanded considerably, to more than 90 offerings by 1964. At the same time scoring and processing were growing, and all indications were that CTB was a thriving business with great potential.

Once the *Progressive Achievement Test* was published in 1933, Willis, Dr. Tiegs, and a Stanford-Binet test specialist, Dr. Elizabeth T. Sullivan, collaborated on "quantifying" a test with similar qualities so it could be used for group testing. The Stanford-Binet was used to test intelligence; however, it had to be administered on an individual basis. The test focused on two distinct areas of intelligence, verbal and nonverbal. The obvious thing would be to call the series "intelligence" tests, but the use of the word "intelligence" in testing was falling into disfavor. After much discussion, they decided to call it "mental maturity." Thus, the *California Test of Mental Maturity* came into being in 1936. In making such a parallel test to be used in classrooms, and incorporating the "articulated, integrated" concept previously established with the *California Achievement Test*, the objective was to administer the two tests together and thereby establish a predictive equation, which they called "anticipated achievement." With this, Willis's goal of establishing case histories for each pupil was slowly becoming a reality and other supportive tests would round out the test catalog.

The *California Achievement Tests* were divided into three major subject areas: Reading, Arithmetic (called Mathematics at the Advanced level), and Language. These were broken down into subtests of Reading Comprehension and Reading Vocabulary, Arithmetic Reasoning and Arithmetic Fundamentals, and Language for the Mechanics of English and Spelling. Willis explained, "These tests provided an 'articulated' series which measured, at appropriate levels, the same basic skills and learning functions, but at increasing levels of difficulty." This made it possible to provide a sequential testing program from grades 1 through 14 in both a statistically scaled and continuous area of content matter. [Junior college was referred to as grades 13 and 14.] Four forms of each level were available, so forms could be alternated for retesting as they were equivalent in content, discriminating power, and difficulty. Achievement test specialists rated the test items themselves for balance and appropriateness by curriculum.

Comprehensive manuals containing both grade placement and percentile norms were available. The manuals also contained data articulated between levels, equivalency studies among forms, studies of comparability with other tests, item studies, reliability and validity studies, and related research information. For those schools wanting to test just one subject area, for example, reading, separate tests were available.

There was also an interesting development related to the packaging of the tests. Other publishers' tests generally were packaged in units of 25 or 50, but when a study showed that the average class size was 35, the *California Achievement Tests* were packaged in units of 35 tests per package. This made it much more convenient for those administering the tests and was a one-up on competitors. A handy conversion chart for ordering in multiples of 35 was included in the catalog. After more than 75 years and a number of updates, the *California Achievement Tests* are still being sold.

The tests were printed, packaged, labeled, and warehoused at the storage company. The equipment was fascinating to watch, and some activities required very skilled workers. There were two linotype machines, and of particular interest to me was one of the operators, a very handsome, dashing young man, but I was too shy to do more than appreciate his smile.

The linotype machine was like a formidable, big iron typewriter and when the keys were pressed, the appropriate typefaces tinkled down a chute and were put into place. Pouring molten lead into reproduced molds created the typefaces. The lead had to be heated to about 550 degrees Fahrenheit, so it was scary to be around and a lot of accidents could happen with flying metal or burns, but the end result was a line of type. Linotypes had been in use since 1886 but are now rare.

There was also an operation that took the printed tests and cut them to packaging size using a gigantic cutting machine, which had a huge blade like a slanted guillotine that could slice through big stacks of paper. Just to watch the operator straighten the stacks with his bare hands before releasing the blade was almost too scary to behold.

The presses were very complicated—the paper had to be stacked to specific measurements, the ink had to be just right, and, of course, the presses had to be in efficient working condition. The sound of the presses could be heard as one approached the building, and there was always a sort of assurance that emanated from the steady, repetitive noise of the platens click-clacking back and forth. Once in a while, the paper stacks would get stuck or shoot off the press, and it was quite a sight to see the pressmen running around trying to stop the press and rescue the run, if possible, with a lot of cussing to help things along.

It was very interesting to watch the bindery workers, a mixed bag of very swift-fingered women who would take the loose tests, count them very fast, wrap them tight so the package wouldn't pop open, and then affix a label. When I worked with them for a while, I discovered this was harder than it looked, and I never was able to wrap packages that didn't eventually pop open. While working at long tables as they processed the tests, the women would exchange X-rated stories and incidents, probably to break the monotony of the job. I learned a lot of four-letter words from those experiences.

Years later, when I became personnel (now "Human Resources") manager, I attended a meeting sponsored by the Department of Vocational Education. The seminar emphasized the unique abilities of certain types of handicapped workers. One segment was devoted to explaining how the deaf could be trained to be skilled at activities requiring dexterity. The noisy bindery seemed to be appropriate for the placement of deaf workers. My discussion with personnel from the Department led to the hiring of several bindery workers and a lead worker who could read lips. Heaven sent? Well, no. The Department failed to mention that there could be resentment on the part of the regular workers at having deaf workers filling similar jobs. The regulars first sulked, then began saying terribly insulting things to the deaf; although they couldn't hear the remarks, they could certainly sense the animosity aimed at them. The regulars did everything they could to block the efficiency of the deaf, even to the point of slacking off on their own work. The deaf workers became very aware of the resentment and hostility building up, and, one by one, they chose to leave CTB. One of the last to go was the lead worker, Madeleine Springer, whom we all had come to admire tremendously. She was a very pretty, intelligent lady who labeled herself as "an unfound treasure," as indeed she was. Her ability to translate directions, first by reading the lips of the supervisor and then passing them to the workers by signing, was fascinating to watch, and she always did it with a smile.

CHAPTER 15

THE CONSULTANTS

There was the growing need for more product recognition, so in the early 1950s Ethel started to investigate some school supply houses to put sales of CTB tests into the hands of schoolbook salesmen who, after all, were calling on the schools anyway. Most of the other test publishers used this avenue for their sales, and this seemed very logical to Ethel. When she told Willis of her plan he, for once, reared back and was absolutely adamant that his tests were not to be sold by "pencil pushers" or book salesmen. His position, unequivocally, was that the tests were constructed by professionals, were normed by professionals, were going to be sold to professionals, and should be represented by professionals.

Ethel begrudgingly gave into this idea, and the end result was one of the most significant steps forward CTB ever took. Ethel and Willis searched to find someone who knew testing and the proper use of test results, and who had at least a master's degree and educational research experience. In 1950 an educational conference was to be held in East Lansing, Michigan, so Willis, Ethel, and Warren set out to see what hope there might be of finding someone to fit Willis's requirements. They were put in touch with John Armstrong, the Director of Research for the State Department of Education in Madison, Wisconsin. John was affable, outgoing, and knowledgeable about tests and measurement in education—just exactly the kind of person they were looking for. Not only that, he liked to have a drink and had a little notebook in which he had the punch lines of what must have been a hundred or more jokes. He was greatly in demand as a speaker, particularly in the Catholic schools market, which was one area where CTB had not made much of an entry. Lots of people thought he looked like Randolph Scott, a well-known actor. Some of his colleagues used to razz him about being "John Armstrong, the all-American consultant."

John's original territory for CTB was the United States, his title was Educational Consultant, and, as you will see, he set the pace and founded the traditions that became the standards for many other educational consultants to follow. One unique aspect, and one that other companies refused to believe, was that the consultants were on straight salary, not commission. Not only that, but if they really felt another company's test better suited the customer's needs, they were encouraged to say so. Not too many businesses looked out for the customer's benefit in such a manner, and their honesty was rewarded.

After John was hired, it became apparent that this was a very good idea, and he was asked to help select another person as near like him as possible. The person turned out to be John (Jim) Hughes, State Director of Guidance in Maine. John and Jim then selected the next consultant, Marlin Schrader, State Director of Occupational Information and Guidance in Kansas, and so it went, growing to fifteen consultants by 1955. Over the years the consultants became a very important advisory group on the kinds of tests needed, improvements on the existing tests, and what supplementary materials would be most helpful. A very close camaraderie grew among the consultants—they really governed themselves, helped each other with difficult customers, and maintained a strong, ethical approach to their work.

With this kind of advisory talent available to the schools without charge, CTB kept growing and Ethel became very aware of the need to support the consultants by locating the test warehousing and scoring services closer to their customers. At that time the only service was in Los Angeles, so customers had to order the tests from there, then ship their answer sheets back to California for processing, and pay the transportation costs.

Using the same technique applied in hiring consultants, after considering the best locations that were also near a consultant, Ethel chose three other areas to be established as warehousing and scoring sites.

The first area to be determined was the Eastern part of the United States, and New Cumberland, Pennsylvania, a small town across the river from Harrisburg, the capital, was chosen as the location for a branch in 1950. Jim Hughes, the closest consultant, was asked to select a branch manager who would stock and ship the tests and establish a test-scoring service. Jim selected a young man who had just graduated from Dickinson University with a major in psychology to serve as branch manager. George Gracey was sent to Los Angeles to receive training in the proper use of test results directly from Willis and Dr. Tiegs. He was also given enough of an introduction to the intricacies of test development and norming to answer the basic questions he would be asked. For more technical questions, he could turn to Jim Hughes.

The war made it difficult to find a proper site. Finally they found an old lodge, formerly a church. George's father bought the place, and he and George worked to clean it up and make it habitable. Later on, they added a small building that was adjacent to the lodge. Even still later, as the branch demands grew, George's father came to the rescue again. He bought contiguous land and doubled the warehouse space they already had. And yes, George's father was reimbursed by CTB for his purchases.

"We had no problem getting scoring help," said George. "New Cumberland had a number of ladies connected with the local Methodist church who were only too happy to have part time jobs as test scorers. They would work through our busy times and then have summers off to be with their families so that tied in perfectly. I found that some strapping boys from nearby Pennsylvania Dutch farmlands with no intention of going further than high school made perfect warehouse help."

"There were lots of visitors, dropping by primarily to see what the test-scoring operation with its new machines was all about. One episode sticks out in my mind," continued George.

> There was a Social Security Administration office close by and one day they called to see if we could help them out with scoring a large overload of their tests and then came down to view what we were doing. Imagine our mutual surprise when three black gentlemen arrived for the preliminary viewing. I could imagine what was going through their mind when they came in and found thirty smiling white faces looking at them. Sure enough, before leaving the head of the group asked if CTB was an

equal opportunity employer. I could honestly say 'yes' and explained the difficulty of hiring non-Caucasians in our area. My explanations must have satisfied them for shortly after their visit a huge vanload of answer sheets arrived and we completed the job with no problems whatsoever.

Lloyd Rensel, a customer affiliated with the University of Dayton, had a test-scoring service for Catholic schools that covered Ohio to New York. He was very important to CTB, ordering thousands of tests and answer sheets, and using New Cumberland scoring services. He was a most congenial man, often bringing priests and other dignitaries to see George's operation. Lloyd once was carting such a large load of tests in the back of his station wagon that it broke down on the nearby turnpike. George had to assist him in getting the car back to town. He arranged for a service mechanic to come off-hours, and he put the car back into working condition by the next day, so Lloyd could keep to his schedule.

Lloyd loved basketball. One time he arranged for the testing schedule in New York City to coincide with the National Invitational Tournament. That way he could combine business with pleasure and had a lot of fun with his colleagues as they watched the games.

CTB established two other branches: one in Madison, Wisconsin, where John Armstrong lived; and the other in Dallas, Texas, near William Robinson, the consultant for that area. The Dallas operation was originally located in the infamous Texas School Book Depository but eventually was moved to larger quarters in Irving, near Dallas. Managers of the branches in Wisconsin (Arthur Maenner) and Texas (Curtis Hamby) had parallel duties to George Gracey in Pennsylvania. They were remarkable men with outstanding personalities, yet all so very different and, at the same time, compatible. Their jobs included customer relations, personnel, and representation in the community, in addition to the warehousing and scoring of CTB tests. Each carried his responsibilities with a sense of pride. Ethel was very fortunate to have three such excellent, dedicated individuals selected by the consultants for these jobs.

The foresight in establishing the branches took an unexpected turn when Ethel had a change of heart regarding staff conferences. To quote from an interview with her:

With the company growing and now with an enlarged consultant staff and branches I felt, and rightly so, that it was necessary to go beyond the U.S. Mail and telephones for a cohesive operation. Remember in those days, there were no computers, no e-mails, no conference calls, so it was decided despite the expense to start holding annual staff conferences. This would provide the professional staff, the consultants and those at the home office to get together to discuss technical information and possible needs relating to the tests, norming and scoring, customer activities and needs.

Staff conferences started out in the 1950s on a very modest basis, held at locations near the home office in Hollywood, where a sense of excitement pervaded in anticipation of the arrival of the renowned consultants. During the conferences, the employees and the consultants were encouraged to get acquainted and discuss special needs with those they were working with and, on the surface, that all seemed to work out pretty well.

Ethel was so enthusiastic about the reception of the consultants in the marketplace that she decided to have a video made about them. The youngest and probably the handsomest consultant was Claude Cunningham, so he was chosen to be the spokesman. Appropriate copy was written and rehearsed. Claude was outfitted in a nice suit, the CTB tie (that all the consultants hated), and an oversized name badge. Many of us, including Ethel, were gathered in the studio to view the taping. Claude was given his cue and began, "My name is . . ." then looked down to his badge for reassurance " . . . Claude Cunningham." The camera stopped. Claude turned white from embarrassment. Ethel absolutely glared at him while the rest of us couldn't contain our laughter—our fabulous consultant who didn't even know his name! Poor Claude never did completely live it down.

It soon became apparent to Ethel that some of the office staff, primarily the females, were attracting more than their share of time from the all-male consultants. On one occasion, several of the ladies got together and planned their own lunch to honor the consultants. Ethel, who learned about it later, was very vocal about her displeasure. This would not do.

In one of the unfortunate episodes that occurred one evening after cocktail hour, a number of consultants participated in a previously established date with some of the office ladies at the home of one of them way up in the Hollywood Hills. The hostess was a free, Bohemian spirit, her place filled with candles, lots of cigarette smoke (Ethel be damned), guitar music, and plenty of booze. The dimly lit front room had a number of mirrors, some facing outdoors, that caused one of the fellows to misjudge distance and go crashing out a window. He ended up badly scratched and bruised. Fortunately a hedge kept him from rolling down the hill. Listening to the explanation the injured consultant gave to Ethel the next day when questioned about his injuries was hilarious when one knew what had actually happened. Of course the consultants considered themselves honor bound not to "rat" on each other, and Ethel was seething.

After a couple more unfortunate episodes, it was decided to hold the conferences elsewhere, away from Los Angeles.

CHAPTER 16

"CALL ME MADAM"

The decision to hold the conferences in a venue other than Los Angeles will go down in the annals of CTB history as among the most memorable and outstanding events of the company. In an effort to increase crowd control and reduce the number of females at these predominantly male events, Ethel decided to try more remote places. One conference was held at the Santa Barbara Biltmore, a hotel with very deluxe accommodations, a nice meeting room, and right across the road from the Pacific Ocean with plenty of opportunities for swims, volleyball, and other recreational activities. However, there was some sort of a misunderstanding over the costs, so in the mid-1950s she decided next to try what was then called the Del Monte Lodge, which was up north in Pebble Beach, the golfing capital of California and maybe the world. The Clarks and Warren had visited there many times for their own getaways from the stress of the business. Since they liked to play golf, they worked that in too.

Ethel thought the Del Monte Lodge was the perfect place for the conferences because it was isolated, and there was no temptation to leave the premises to go elsewhere. Of course, she was very wrong about this because people will be people. It didn't take long for the consultants to discover that Carmel was about four miles away and that the Mission Ranch was about the only really lively place in town. It had great music and dancing and a wonderful piano bar at which people could stand and sing. Several of the fellows really had beautiful voices and one in particular, Dr. Robert Hoey from Texas, liked to sing "Lida Rose" from the "Music Man." It got to be his claim to fame, and everybody would harmonize with him. It was great fun!

The Del Monte Lodge was set up differently in the 1950s than it is now. Instead of a large restaurant there were smaller tables, and each person had to write down his or her order for food. This took place at breakfast and dinner and was handled just as it used to be in the dining cars during the days of luxury railroad travel. Some of the more devilish consultants would have great fun mixing up the written orders and room numbers, much to the dismay of the waitresses, and I'm pretty sure they were happy to see us leave each year.

It seems doubtful that Ethel ever realized that there were outings after the dinners at the lodge and that the fellows did not just obediently go to bed. Her master plan of prohibiting wives from attending the conferences because they might cause possible distractions from the business at hand was certainly thwarted by all the post-dinner machinations—sort of an unspoken joke on Ethel.

In those days the Del Monte Lodge had adequate rooms for the CTB meetings held on a daily basis. Conferences usually lasted about five days, and could be a real trial. The heavy drinking sometimes impaired the progress of the meetings. John Armstrong always had a saying that "any old horse can stay up all night, but it takes a thoroughbred to get up in the morning" and that was sure the way it was many times. On a particularly memorable occasion, despite the requirement of mandatory attendance at nine o'clock in the morning for the professional part of the conference, one of the star consultants by the name of Marlin Schrader really had gone overboard and just was not going to make it by nine o'clock. His buddies came to the rescue—they wrapped toilet paper around one of his sleeves and put a great big red cross on it, then literally dragged him half-conscious into the meeting room and put him in a chair, so he made the time constraint after all!

Aside from the business meetings, the daily big event began in the evenings after the working sessions had ended. At five o'clock all the consultants were expected to attend (Expected to attend? No, it was mandatory!) a cocktail party that was focused on telling dirty jokes. Now Ethel was a very earthy woman who loved her drinks. She also loved men and she loved dirty jokes, so it became a contest each evening to see who could tell the "best" or, I guess one would say, the dirtiest joke. In the early days of the conferences these sessions were pretty tame, but as more and more conferences were held and as the consultant numbers grew, these "parties" were, depending on one's viewpoint, either hilarious or despicable times. There were actually occasions where some of the fellows really wanted to get up and leave because of the kinds of stories that were being told, but no one dared because of Ethel and so they stayed.

The cocktail parties were very important to Ethel. She would spend about an hour or so before the party getting ready. She would make a grand entrance after most of the fellows were there, and the party would begin. She actually saw herself as a second Ethel Merman and wanted to purport herself with the same sort of crass comments and conduct, with constant references to Merman's role in *Call Me Madam*. In one of her favorite party sayings related to Willis and me, when asked why she only had one child, she would say about Willis, "He tried it once, and didn't like it." Willis never even blinked.

CHAPTER 17

THE IBM 1401

In the 1950s there were five major test-publishing companies. Four of them were conducted as regular businesses, but Educational Testing Services, operating out of Princeton, New Jersey, had a nonprofit status. The fact they did not have to pay taxes on income gave them a distinct competitive advantage. Their main market was the college-bound student, and they developed and published the *Scholastic Aptitude Test* (SAT), which was and still is used throughout the U.S., primarily as a precollege entrance exam. They administered, scored, and reported the SAT test results, but they also published a small offering of tests in the elementary market that were in direct competition with the other publishers' tests. It was this tax-free segment of their business that enraged Willis. It seemed grossly unfair to him that CTB should have to pay taxes while ETS did not on similar products.

He got nowhere trying to contact ETS various times about the discrepancy. He decided to contact an organization that had specialists in the nonprofit unrelated business income tax area, known familiarly as UBIT. The specialists there agreed with Willis that ETS had an unfair economic advantage, but nothing was going to change without legal action. Willis was adamant that the unequal playing field be leveled. CTB proceeded with confronting what seemed an insurmountable obstacle. A man named Harry Wardenberg from Arthur Andersen Company was hired by CTB to see this case through the various legal channels. He ended up with a Congressional hearing and a vote in favor of CTB's position that was entered into the Congressional Record. Harry was such a hero to CTB that Ethel hired him as Financial Vice-President. He was handsome, charming, and impressive, which probably influenced Ethel to ramrod his acceptance into the CTB hierarchy. He no doubt was a relief to both Maurice Wilson, then Treasurer of CTB, and to Willis, who were both continually on the lookout for various ways to help alleviate CTB's tax burden. It was through Harry and his influence on Willis and Ethel that CTB eventually embarked on a company-wide profit sharing plan. He helped Willis establish the Willis W. Clark Foundation as a nonprofit entity focusing on educational research.

Piracy by unauthorized users has been a continuing problem for publishers, and test publishers are not immune to "borrowing." When CTB tests were sold only in booklet form there was some abuse. A number of educators took advantage of the "fair use" doctrine. Fair use is a doctrine in United States copyright law that allows limited use of copyrighted material without requiring permission from the rights holders, such as for commentary, criticism, news reporting, research, teaching, or scholarship. It provides for the legal, non-licensed citation or incorporation of copyrighted material in another author's work under a four-factor balancing test. The abusers took the questions from the tests and reprinted them for their own use without permission. This was an outright violation of CTB's copyrights, going way beyond the fair use doctrine. It also distorted the carefully constructed norming samples.

The problem was exacerbated by the advent of the test-scoring machine. Three pieces were needed to test each student: the test booklet, the answer sheet, and the norms. The norms enabled the user to convert the raw scores, which were obtained by processing the answer sheet through the test-scoring machine, into meaningful data. There wasn't too much trouble with the booklets themselves, but the answer sheets and norms were pilfered with impunity. Sometimes schools simply made up their own answer sheets to be used with the booklets by using overlay stencils to hand-score their answer sheets. They used the norms in the manual for conversion, claiming the answer sheets were not copyrightable. The worst offenders were those who took the norms and applied them in the equivalent of their own machine scoring service. The norms were what made the test comparisons or predictions meaningful but were extremely time consuming and costly to produce. CTB had to protect their trustworthiness and its investment.

CTB consulted several intellectual property rights attorneys and finally settled upon Caspar Weinberger, who at the time was active in California politics. Weinberger later served as U.S. Secretary of Health, Education, and Welfare under Presidents Nixon and Ford, and he served as U.S. Secretary of Defense under President Reagan. Incredibly enough, ETS had hired him for practically the same reasons, so both parties were encouraged that we might strengthen our position. Weinberger obtained a ruling that the answer sheets were part of the test and thus were covered by the copyright laws. It was a major victory. Later CTB developed a licensing form granting permission to school districts to use its norms when processing the answer sheets, charging a royalty per sheet processed. The school districts objected. Morton Goldberg, an attorney who was a star in the intellectual properties arena, was retained and his assistance settled the validity of licensing for use of the norms.

In 1956, another settlement that affected CTB was reached. IBM settled by consent decree a long-standing anti-trust lawsuit brought by the U.S. Department of Justice. IBM's monopolies were broken up, and their patents, leases, and other controlling methods were required to be abandoned.

CTB's scanner operations had seen the transition from processing a student's answers on a mark-sense card to a large answer sheet format that could capture a great many more responses on a single sheet. This led to much shorter scoring and processing times, but it was of mixed benefit for the lower grades. The students had to mark their answers on very long sheets, which had to be unfolded individually and stretched to an arm's length before they could be processed. However, the mostly female scoring staff concluded that this practice, however tedious, was worth the effort in the long run because of the potential for bust enlargement.

Eventually a department called Copyrights and Permissions was established at CTB to handle incoming requests for the use of test items for special purposes and to seek permission for CTB authors and editors to use certain items from other publishers. Because of my long experience dealing with these problems, the responsibility for the department became mine.

As time went on, our scoring and processing services grew and grew. (See the Appendix for details.) Of course it was necessary to keep our equipment up-to-date and Ethel, having neither knowledge of nor interest in the machines, turned the acquisitions and operations over to individuals who came with high recommendations. It speaks well for those selected because very good coordination with the services being offered at our branches was required. In the early days the operators had to do their own programming, an art form in its own right. Later on, both the answer forms and equipment for scoring and processing became more sophisticated (and more expensive), and the demands on the operators began to require around-the-clock shifts.

The acquisition of the IBM 1401 in 1961 saw the installation of the first real computer, which completely revolutionized the way CTB processed tests and provided scoring and reporting products. Many of us, including me, were in awe of its powers.

Probably a bit fed up with all the fanfare, Ed Wright, one of the managers, put things into perspective when he said that people have a tendency to think of the machines as brains that were going to solve all their problems. He said, "They are far from being brains. Machines are actually very stupid. They don't do anything at all until you tell them what to do. You've got to do the thinking. They don't compare in any way with the human mind because the human mind reasons and draws conclusions." He said that the only advantage the machines had was fantastic memory with almost immediate recall. He emphasized that the IBM machine was not going to solve all our problems.

Well, Ed was right about the problem solving. CTB had so much business coming in from the schools that the promised turnaround time began to be a real detriment. Answer sheets and other forms to be serviced were really pouring in. One of the supervisors at the time solved the problem to his satisfaction. He simply boxed up a lot of the forms waiting their turn and put them up in the mezzanine to get them out of the way, and then forgot about them. When Ethel found out about this she fired him on the spot. I wonder what her reaction would have been if she knew there was the occasional poker game and many a bottle of booze passed around during the long boring runs at night.

CHAPTER 18

NORTH!

I probably should have foreseen the move. Starting about 1954, Ethel's problems with her allergy to the sun inaugurated a series of vacations to the Monterey Peninsula. She and Willis became quite familiar with the beauty of the area and considered which properties there might be suitable for them.

The three of them, Ethel, Willis, and Warren, began visiting the Monterey Peninsula more frequently, looking for property on which to build a vacation home. It was a most intensive search since there were so many lovely spots available for building at that time. They had to decide whether to be close to the heart of the city or out on the coastline of Pebble Beach. Ethel stated her viewpoint in this manner, "There is only so much land adjacent to water in the whole world, so why shouldn't we enjoy a piece of it!" That became the focus of the search.

They placed the responsibility for finding a home site in the hands of a realtor connected to Del Monte Properties, the company established by Samuel F. B. Morse, one of the early developers of Pebble Beach. The realtor's name was Jack Neville. He was a golf celebrity who had helped develop the Pebble Beach Golf Course. He also knew many people who lived there, which was important to Ethel. Jack found them a gorgeous location on Pebble Beach's picturesque 17-Mile Drive with an unobstructed view looking out over the ocean, as well as a view of Cypress Point with its famous golf course. The Clarks retained the architect Robert Jones to draw up the plans with the stipulation that every room have a view of the ocean and that the home be on one floor. One floor was important because neither Ethel nor Willis wanted to cope with stairs as they had in Hollywood. Ethel made modifications to the plans—she truly had a flair for design that was reflected in the rather ingenious alterations she made involving built-in furniture and a galley-type kitchen with an indoor stone barbecue.

They hired a well-known contractor, Miles Bain, who had an impeccable reputation for strict adherence to detail, and then they returned home to Hollywood. It was more than a six-hour drive from Hollywood to the new building site. It fell on Warren to visit there periodically to check how things were progressing. It was one more example of how effectively Ethel could use any of us, Willis, Warren, or me as her spokesperson; then if things didn't work out, she could transfer the blame to whomever she had given the responsibility—in this case, Warren.

The Clarks eventually met General Waldron, who lived close to the building site. They worked out a deal with him: he would stay in contact with Warren and serve as on-site overseer of the project. Ethel's interest perked up when she found out a general was in the act, and her visits to the site increased.

The Pebble Beach house was finally finished in 1958 and was far beyond expectations. Cannell and Chapin, a Los Angeles interior-decorating firm furnished it. It was ultimately featured in the local paper, the Monterey Herald. Many of the homes in Pebble Beach have names, so Ethel searched for just the right one. Her grandson, Tim, came up with "Ebb Tide," from the title of a popular song of that time. Ethel thought it was perfect, as the song recording featured sea gulls calling and waves crashing in the background. Ethel embraced the name. The house was christened with that name, an appropriate sign was made, stationery was produced, and many decorative accents on the theme were purchased.

I remember a time at Ebb Tide, with its panoramic views of the Pacific Ocean and several holes of Cypress Point Golf Course, where President Dwight D. Eisenhower was playing one day. One of the greens is visible from an Ebb Tide bathroom. Mother said, "I may be the only woman in America who can sit on the can and see the President 4-putt."

In Los Angeles, the crowded situation at CTB and the inability to locate a suitable facility for the growing staff was of increasing concern. It became obvious that some sort of arrangement had to be made to relocate either some or all of the company. The thought finally took root in Ethel's mind that as long as they were spending so much time in Pebble Beach, why not move the company there. She was totally enamored with the area and so enthusiastic about it that she and Willis met with a representative of Del Monte Properties (DMP) to discuss a move. It turned out that DMP was in the process of planning the Del Monte Research Park, next to the Monterey Peninsula Airport. DMP was looking for just the right company to become the first occupant. The Del Monte Research Park was to be used strictly for research and scientifically oriented operations. Test development and publishing fit the bill perfectly. DMP would subrogate the property. Ethel was ecstatic. She began to formulate plans quickly, never imagining that any of the employees down in the hot, smoggy Los Angeles area would not leap at the chance to relocate to the Monterey Peninsula with its clean air and scenic beauty. They could all move together.

With not much more investigation than that, Ethel was determined to go ahead with building the new facility. She ignored Willis and Shanner's cautions that they were in the middle of a costly and time-consuming dual re-standardization of the *California Achievement Test* and the *California Test of Mental Maturity*. The re-standardization was necessitated by the change in the school curriculum as a result of Sputnik and the newly emphasized requirements for added training in mathematics and science. These changes had a direct effect on the norms, which unfortunately had just been established a year or two earlier and now had to be revised. The monetary strain on the firm to come out with the earlier edition of the norms was doubly stretched now that all the work had to be done again.

Even more specifically, CTB was basically a mail-order house, Los Angeles being one of the four branches serving as warehousing, shipping, and receiving for both the tests themselves and the accompanying scoring and reporting services. It is doubtful that any kind of an investigation of shipping and delivery facilities or the available workforce in the Monterey area was ever undertaken. Ethel never gave heed to any of these serious obstacles.

Despite her disregard of certain aspects of the company, Ethel did care strongly about the welfare of the employees. In an interview in the 1960s, when she was asked why she felt it wise to provide the employees with so many benefits in addition to their salaries, Ethel replied:

None of us can do a good job if we are worried about the health of our families or about what would become of our families if we were to become ill. We all need security; we or no company can promise its employees a job forever but we can give them a feeling of security as long as they are employed and doing their work well.

As the company has grown and we could afford more benefits we have tried to provide more and more security for our employees. I guess we have been pioneers in the field. I know we were among the first companies to pay the whole bill for the employees' health and hospitalization coverage. Of course that is fairly common practice today but we have done it for years. We were also among the first to grant birthdays off with pay if they fell on a working day. I guess this practice has also spread. Very few companies worked less than a forty-hour week when we started our 38-3/4 hour week.

We have added to the benefits until today I think we have everything pretty well covered. We have the health and hospitalization. On top of that we added the major medical in case of a serious or long illness that today costs a pile of money. There is cheap life insurance available through the company. Every employee, if he is ill and unable to work, is entitled to 70 percent of his pay each week for one year. I think there is a maximum on this of $65 but that is a good feeling knowing that some money would be coming in to meet the food and rent expenses if an employee were to become ill.

And, of course, we are real proud of the employees' profit sharing retirement trust since this provides the means for an employee to accumulate a lot of money for future retirement. You know that the company puts a third of its profits into the trust each year it makes a profit. But naturally it has to make a profit to be able to do so. This fund has grown fast.

So for every regular employee, we have provided security against illness, against loss of income in case of illness, insurance protection for the families, and savings for retirement. I don't know what more we can do but we are always keeping our eyes open and keep trying to improve.

Then, too, as an employee stays with the company or his responsibilities increase, we endeavor to have his salary go up, and as it does he is entitled to even more benefits since he or she becomes even more important to the continuing success of the company.

When asked, "Just what do you expect from CTB employees in return for their salaries and all these benefits?" Ethel replied:

> I expect them to know their job and go ahead and do it. Don't be afraid to take on new jobs or more work. If you don't hear from me, you're doing a good job. If you hear from me, look out. I'd like to go around and say 'hello' to everyone every day, but if I did—there's just not that many hours in a day, so I can't do it. Over the years, I've attempted to visit the CTB family all around the country because I felt the families in the field needed me.

In response to another question, "Some young people today seem to be afraid of work. How do you feel about this? How much work do you expect of the employees?" Ethel replied:

> Roll up your sleeves and work. If you have a united front, you will really make something for yourself. I made a promise that when your profit sharing trust gets big enough and you want this building, go ahead and have it and pay yourselves rent. But that would include all the field people too. Don't forget about them. We have an administrative committee and then we have an investment committee to consider such things for the benefit of the profit sharing trust. The point I'm trying to make is that there are plenty of opportunities here at CTB. But it's up to all of you to work hard for them to make them reality. Nothing comes easy. The continued growth of this company depends for the most part on your hard work. Decide what you want out of life and go after it. All we can do is assure you that

we plan to keep the company going. Now it is up to you to make it grow and prosper.

When asked if she had any advice about what she'd like to see done with the company in the years ahead, Ethel responded:

> Well, that's a difficult question. I've always had faith in youth. In the old days I was the personnel manager. It was quite amusing. I don't know how many thousands of young men I've interviewed. My first word of advice was to keep going to school. The minute you stop there are 1,000 other young men that are going to go right past you. If you stop learning and concentrate on deep heating a baby's bottle, why, I've got news for you. You're going to come to me in about a year from now and want a raise and you're not going to get it because the other man had been going ahead with their learning while you heated the milk. We've always tried to emphasize the 'go ahead of the individual.' We also have no retirement age in this company. It's your ability that counts.

She was then asked, "Your main point then is whether the person is producing or not?" Ethel said:

> That's right, whether they produce or not. You shouldn't be urged to produce. You should all join hands and realize that you have to produce if you want to get ahead. What can you lose? If you do join hands and all work together—that means the branches, that means all of you sitting here, that means everybody—others will be looking to you for leadership. What we, as management, would like to do would be to think of high policy matters only. It's up to you to carry out the ideas or policies. Now I'd like to make a pledge to you. CTB will always stand behind you if you continue to learn and go up the ladder. I'm sure you all will, but it is up to you as individuals.

CHAPTER 19

MONTEREY

Ethel was very excited about moving the company to Monterey. She turned to Jack Neville and to others with DMP for help in selecting an architect and contractor for the new building to be located in the Del Monte Research Park, as the area was called at that time. She came up with well-known and respected individuals with excellent credentials: Ted Minnis, architect, and Joseph Fratessa, contractor. They teamed up to keep everything on schedule and on budget. Cannell and Chapin, a Los Angeles interior-decorating firm, was hired to finish the interiors. The exceptionally large front offices were extremely impressive, giving them an aura of prestige that Ethel loved. The local newspaper, The Monterey Peninsula Herald, ran this headline and story of the impending move:

$3 Million Testing Center in Monterey

A $3 million-a-year business will move its national headquarters from Los Angeles to Monterey this year. California Test Bureau, one of the country's biggest and oldest publishers of educational and psychological test materials, announced today that it expects to move into a new building on the Salinas Highway about Sept. 1. The firm said it plans to relocate 100 of its professional and technical staff, with their families, on the Peninsula during the next several months. Mrs. Ethel M. Clark, president of California Test Bureau . . .

One of the important and pressing issues was notifying the employees about the opportunities and what they could mean for them and their families. Ethel sent the following letter to all the employees, outlining what was going to happen and telling them about a meeting that would be held to explain things in more detail.

 CALIFORNIA TEST BUREAU
5916 HOLLYWOOD BLVD.   HOllywood 3-2384
LOS ANGELES 28, CALIFORNIA

TO: All Regular Los Angeles Employees of CTB

FROM: Ethel M. Clark, President

DATE: February 3, 1960

SUBJECT: Future Location of CTB

Your management has, of yesterday, reached a definite decision to have the Del Monte Properties Company construct a new office building and warehouse for CTB at the Del Monte Research Park in Monterey, California. This decision was reached after literally hundreds of hours of research and deliberation by a committee from our management plus outside advisers. This decision is, we sincerely believe, in the best interests of the company and each of you who are such an important part of its well-being. In essence, the Del Monte Properties Company has offered us a proposition whereby CTB can purchase its own building on three acres of land for its new headquarters location.

We extend to each of you the invitation to move with the company to its new location and share with us what we hope will be an even more prosperous future and a happy life.

Within a few days, each of you will receive an invitation for you and your husband or wife to attend a dinner meeting at a local hotel. At that meeting we plan to explain in detail the company plans for moving as well as its plans for assisting you in moving your households. We shall also during the evening provide you with more information concerning the Monterey Peninsula and what you may expect to find in the way of housing and facilities.

Our new building will be ready for occupancy about September 1, 1960. This allows all of us several months to make adequate preparations. For that reason, we ask you to continue to exercise for a few more days the admirable patience you have shown us during these months of deliberations. We are certain that you and your families will feel more assured after having attended the dinner meeting. And we hope that after this meeting each and every one of you will decide to share with us this new experience.

This move represents an important and difficult decision, but one which had to be made in order to keep pace with CTB's continuing progress and growth. We have enjoyed the Monterey Peninsula for many years and are enthusiastic about the plans for our new business home. I sincerely hope and believe that you will share our enthusiasm, and will continue to contribute your fine efforts which have made, and will make, this vital move possible.

706 BRIDGE STREET, NEW CUMBERLAND, PA.   •   110 S. DICKINSON STREET, MADISON 3, WIS.   •   2114 IRVING BLVD., DALLAS 7, TEXAS

Ethel held the meeting at the Hollywood Roosevelt Hotel and invited all the employees and their families. Representatives from Del Monte Properties as well as several dignitaries from Monterey attended the meeting to extol the virtues of the move. She offered all employees two weeks off with pay and expenses to visit the Monterey Peninsula in order to scout the area and get a feel for the location. Almost all the employees accepted the offer, although she was surprised when some employees spurned it. She was more disappointed when she learned some employees took advantage of the offer to have a family vacation in Monterey without having any intention of moving. It was inconceivable to her that some people simply did not want to move to Monterey.

Still others, who initially intended to make the move, looked over the location and changed their minds. The net result was that only one third of the 160 employees agreed to move. Most of these were professional staff. Only a handful of the scoring and reporting group agreed to move. It was quite daunting that there were so few experienced employees available to meet the new opening date of September 1, 1960, which was the beginning of the scoring season. At that point, CTB had a bare minimum of trained staff.

Ethel immediately searched for a personnel manager to help me with hiring new personnel. It was fortunate that the Naval Postgraduate School (NPS) was close by, and many of the wives of NPS students were available for part-time work. However, a tremendous amount of training was necessary. It was a credit to Ethel's persuasive charm that so many of the employees who did move were willing to pitch in and help train the new employees and keep the business going. Ethel could often get her way simply by imposing the sheer force of her will on other people. Yet this was not always the case. In countless instances others were willing to help her because they were attracted to her and enjoyed working with her.

We eventually did sell our new home, and we moved to Monterey, where I stayed with our two children while Frank remained in Culver City and leased out his property. In the meantime, he had purchased a Beechcraft Bonanza plane so he could fly up and visit on occasion. He also could fly to Las Vegas or to Golden Gate Fields for horse racing, so it was not all that bad for him—and he didn't have to see Ethel.

Things went along well and he was able to grow his auto rental business, eventually leasing a large area for his cars at the Monterey Peninsula Airport. Through his contacts he met the local postmaster, who was in need of backup rental cars, and that led to post office rentals and repairs throughout Northern California. He loved his plane and eventually moved up to a better, faster model. He didn't fly for the joy of being in the "wild blue yonder," but rather to "get there fast." I learned how to navigate but had a tendency toward airsickness, which limited my flying hours. Besides, his passion of going back and forth to racetracks was not my thing.

It was ironic that Frank, who took meticulous care of his plane and was an excellent pilot, should die in a return trip from the Golden Gate racetrack in 1986. I have replayed that tragedy over and over in my mind. It was uncertain whether he had a stroke or a heart attack, but he had called in from Moss Landing to say he was en route to Monterey and wasn't feeling well. His plane crashed and burned just short of the Monterey runway.

CHAPTER 20

THE BLUEBIRD OF HAPPINESS

As others often pointed out, my mother's directness could make her particularly difficult to be with. One never had to guess what she meant. It was this very directness that allowed her to break through what today is called the "glass ceiling" at a time when women never got a view of what was beyond that ceiling. She could be infuriating and irrepressible, irritating and irresistible, and she could stand head-to-head with Teamsters and IRS auditors without backing down. She was as sharp as a tack and as tactless as an eyewitness news reporter sticking a microphone in your face.

Ethel was also a gorgeous woman. Today's obsession with beauty and celebrity would certainly place her among the "beautiful people." Her life style would have made her the subject of countless magazine articles and a favorite of shows such as *Entertainment Tonight*. She always kept up with current fashion. She created quite a stir when she appeared in public wearing men's pants a la Marlene Dietrich instead of skirts. She was aware of the latest hairstyles, and her hair was always styled professionally. She believed in keeping herself up with regular facials, massages, and manicures. She had lovely hands, which she used in a very expressive fashion. One day she was at a luncheon at a downtown hotel when a man came up to her and began admiring her hands. He was a sculptor who had been commissioned to do a Venus-type statue to be featured in a prominent spot at the entrance of the hotel. He persuaded Ethel to sit for him. It is not known what happened to the sculpture, but it pleased Ethel to have been selected.

Ethel's tastes became more sophisticated as the company grew and prospered. As CTB began to grow she realized she had an image to maintain, so she paid even more attention to her appearance and to her wardrobe. She decided to change hairdressers and switched to the House of Westmore on Sunset Boulevard. The famous Westmore brothers were make-up artists for Warner Bros. Studios. The salon provided spa services. The Westmores also did make-up for the general public, so Ethel patronized the shop often. She was even more glamorous when she was professionally made-up.

She carried her new approach to her appearance to her clothing with lovely dresses and shoes to match along with several furs. She began having dresses made for her and patronized the more expensive shops. All of this was costing more than it did in the old days, so she tried to do something about that by claiming her clothes were directly related to the business and therefore should be tax deductible as a business expense. Her claim to the IRS was denied but only after she put up a long and determined effort to have it be substantiated.

One time at a convention in Atlantic City, we were coming down an elevator. Ethel was beautifully dressed and perfumed, and a very handsome gentleman entered the elevator and was immediately taken with Ethel's appearance. He never stopped staring at her all the way down to the main floor. As he stood aside to let her exit the elevator, he most admiringly said, "I don't know what you've got, lady, but you sure got it!"

It was at the same convention that some of the consultants decided to surprise her. When she entered the lounge for the cocktail hour, she was presented with a bouquet of flowers. Then she was escorted to a person in the group who was introduced as the Mayor of Atlantic City. He said a few gracious words about her visit and the company and then presented her with the key to the city. Much to her disappointment he had to leave right away because of scheduling problems. She was pleased and excited to have received such a reception, and it is doubtful that she ever realized that the "Mayor" was a man one of the consultants had paid to put on this little charade.

She had a bit of a weight problem, which she mentioned continuously, often at breakfast. She loved oatmeal. One day while she was eating a large bowl of oatmeal, she casually mentioned how much she liked the cereal. Willis, with his dry sense of humor, said, "Back on the farm we used to feed oatmeal to the hogs to fatten them up," and then went on to another subject. I often wondered if Willis had waited for the moment or said it spontaneously. Obviously that took care of Ethel's fondness for oatmeal.

My mother's love of dogs was almost legendary. She nursed them tenderly as if they were little children. As poor little Homer, the Boston Bull Terrier, was always shivering and shaking, Ethel would wrap him in flannel to keep him warm and feed him a special concoction she made of lamb, rice, and carrots that was supposed to keep him healthy. Surprisingly those ingredients form the basis for many commercial dog food products today and are considered important for good nutrition for dogs.

Over the years the breed of Ethel's dogs varied, from a Boston Bull Terrier to a wire-haired Wire Fox Terrier, to a pair of beautiful Golden Cocker Spaniels named Millicent and Not Millicent, to a group of puppies she purchased to represent different countries she visited in Europe. Thus she had an Irish setter she called Molly O'Brien, a Jack Russell Terrier named Jack London, and a Toy Poodle named Louise, after Maurice Chevalier's famous song. At one point she had seven dogs, six of which were controlled by the miserable little poodle Louise. Louise was the alpha dog in Ethel's menagerie. She had an unpleasant disposition that she often displayed by snarling and growling at anyone who came close to Ethel. She sat on Ethel's bed, acting protective, which Ethel seemed to enjoy and encourage. Ethel, to her credit, acted responsibly towards her dogs, going so far as to set up a trust fund to care for them after her death.

Ethel even worried about the deer that roamed so freely in the area of Pebble Beach near her home. She thought they were not finding enough food to survive periods of drought. She had bales of hay brought to her house and spread out for the deer. Some neighbors took exception to this practice, believing it wasn't in the neighborhood's or the deer's best interest because it affected their natural feeding habits. She elicited the help of the SPCA to back her position but that organization sidestepped the issue and didn't help her. Opposition to her practice of feeding the deer escalated until Pebble Beach Company officials got into the fray, and she finally stopped feeding the deer.

Earlier in her life, my mother had become very active in the SPCA, calling with advice and sending financial support. Everyone was under the impression that she had left a substantial sum of money to the organization to become available upon her death. SPCA officials wined and dined her when she got older and wasn't able to leave the house. SPCA members would visit and bring her flowers and candy. She always accepted their gifts with grace and dignity. Following her death, representatives from the SPCA visited her trustee to arrange for the receipt of the bequest to them. It was then they discovered she had canceled her bequest. The cancellation was put into effect about the time of the deer-feeding incident.

There is a story, perhaps apocryphal, that after moving to Pebble Beach Ethel decided it would be a good idea to be associated with a church in order to be more accepted into Pebble Beach society. The motive could have been Willis's failing health, or perhaps, even some insight into her own emotional condition that caused Ethel to move towards a church community. Regardless of the reason, the Clarks decided to join the All Saints Episcopal Church in Carmel.

Ethel's usual approach to becoming prominent in any endeavor was the promise of money, and the potential for large sums of money played a major role in all that happened after they joined All Saints. It did not take long for Ethel, in her flamboyant manner, to march into the church and attempt to monopolize the Pastor as well as be critical of some of the rituals. The church's aged, sedate, and devoted congregation, mostly women, adhered to the ritualistic framework of All Saints. They organized a group to oppose her by complaining to the Reverend Peter Farmer about her attitude and actions. Ethel, true to her colorful nature, inadvertently played into their hands. She decided at Christmastime to send some of the church members a card that expressed her feelings about the group opposing her. The card she selected, that was absolutely hilarious to her, depicted a little bluebird hovering over a pie decorated with holly carrying the message: "May the Bluebird of Happiness Crap on Your Christmas Pie." That did it! The outraged group of ladies approached Reverend Farmer and demanded that Ethel, and Willis by extension, be removed from the church. Some would say it was the Reverend's job to counsel Ethel and try to help her with her un-Christian approach to problem solving, but he did not counsel her and she was asked to leave. Ethel got even. She was deeply hurt by being ostracized. She sent a card to each member of the protesting group. There was no message on the card but when it was opened, there appeared a replica of the third finger, upright and at attention.

CHAPTER 21

THE UNRAVELING

Willis began stretching himself too thinly between working with the test development aspects and getting more and more involved in the day-to-day operations of CTB. He had managed to keep himself in good shape throughout his life. He had a habit of pulling at his hair when he was in deep thought, and the habit began manifesting itself increasingly as he took on more responsibilities. He began having bouts of dizziness, which he tried to keep to himself, but one day while playing golf he collapsed on the golf course. He was rushed to the hospital for tests, which indicated his carotid arteries were filled with plaque. He needed an operation, perhaps on both sides of his neck. This was not good news at anytime, especially because it was regarding his health, but the news came at a time when the dual standardization was in full swing.

To make matters worse, other problems arose over the bank financing. CTB had an excellent relationship with the local bank, which had been so helpful in establishing a line of credit for CTB. When Crocker Bank purchased the local bank the new bank administrator requested a meeting with Ethel and Willis. The administrator, Ray Smith, told them the bank was withdrawing the line of credit. He allowed no room for discussion, telling my parents, "That was it!" Smith and his associates knew nothing about the testing business, so it came as a double shock—no more credit and a closed mind not listening to reason.

The Clarks searched for a new bank. The California Bank had just opened in Monterey and was more than willing to work with Willis and Ethel. However, there is little doubt that the decision of Crocker

Bank had a devastating effect on Willis and seriously exacerbated his deteriorating health.

*   *   *

I have a perspective now of those events that I didn't have then. Perhaps it was being back at CTB again where it all began. I can look around at the highly developed Ryan Ranch area, which is populated by companies that probably didn't exist when my mother decided that this was where she was going to relocate her penny postcard company. I can see events that could not be changed no matter how much I tried.

Perhaps I would have been able to foresee the disenchantment some CTB officers had about the company—their concern provided the impetus to try to spin off from CTB, as if it were a 1950s sitcom. About 1963, four key executives—Ben Rees, Ed Wright, Tom Fitzgibbons, and Bill Melton—contacted a former CTB employee, Bill Gay, who worked for Howard Hughes. When Ethel learned of their mutinous plans, she fired them on the spot. Gay started a division he called Hughes Dynamics without Howard Hughes' knowledge. Along with the four former CTB employees, he created a testing company. Hughes found out about it and abruptly shut it down, but not before many dollars were spent on building remodeling and equipment for the new testing company. The former CTB employees were left without jobs and had to scramble to find new positions.

Nothing is secret very long within a group of people. The breakaway, together with outside forces gossiping about CTB's condition, certainly abetted the general confusion and uncertainty. I'm sure I could not have headed that off, but now it is easy to understand that we had two principals in declining physical and mental health, that CTB was a testing company caught up in an expensive re-norming of their two major tests, and that there were only a few employees with long-standing loyalty to the company. There was realistic worry about what the future would be for everyone involved with CTB. Various appraisers and analysts were making predictions that added to the nervousness of educational and field staff. The breakaway was the catalyst that made everyone begin to look out for himself, as a myriad of uncertain possible scenarios began to arise. Just as parents act unselfishly to protect their children from the outrageous misfortunes of life, I would have acted to ward off the shocking events my own parents were encountering.

The persons who jumped ship to go to Hughes had been in touch with some of the professional field staff about the local situation, which increased the level of tension at CTB. In good faith Ethel and Willis brought in a management consultant, William Howard Church, to review the financial and professional situations with the goal of making necessary improvements. At that time, Dr. Donald Denum, an educator from Texas, also was brought in to help shore up some of the test development operations and close apparent gaps in communication. Church surveyed the staff and came up with recommendations to allegedly help Willis. But Church did not divulge that he and Denum had teamed up and developed plans to take over CTB. It was an unforgivable breach of trust.

I know that nothing I could have said would have prevented Ethel from extending her all-out support to Church and Denum, who constantly flattered her. She was totally unaware of their inadequacies and duplicity. However, the field staff became aware of the Church/Denum proposed coup and became apprehensive about it. They had good cause because they not only had stock in CTB but were members of the profit sharing trust and felt the company would fall apart with a traitor such as Denum running it.

Some of the field staff formed a group to make their own proposal to Willis and Ethel. They offered to buy the company, presenting substantial reasons why this would work to the benefit and perpetuation of CTB. The group, representing the field staff, met with Ethel and Willis at their home to discuss the possibilities. However, as good as their presentation sounded, the reality was they had no financial stability or reserves. It seemed they were turning to my parents for financial support but were not taking into consideration that the Clarks would expect compensation for all their years and years of hard work and would not simply give the company away.

It was at this time in the 1960s that teaching machines were coming into vogue, with the need for software for the new technical equipment. It occurred to some of the hardware companies that CTB's tests would blend nicely with teaching software and would be the perfect addition to their educational equipment. As word spread of CTB's problems, several companies approached Ethel and Willis about buying the company, but none had goals or purposes compatible with those of CTB.

In 1963 it was becoming evident that selling the company would be a viable option. Fortuitously, Paul Lee, one of my parent's longtime friends and an auditor for CTB, learned that McGraw-Hill might be interested in pursuing the purchase of CTB.

Willis's health continued to deteriorate. He began complaining of throat irritation but kept refusing to go to the hospital. His doctors eventually performed carotid artery surgery. Naturally Ethel visited him every day in the hospital and stayed with him as long as she could. During one visit, the chair she was sitting in collapsed underneath her. She broke her leg when she fell to the floor. This created a major crisis in the hospital. My parents were hospitalized at the same time. Ethel raised hell over the situation. Her anger was mitigated only when employees came to visit her after work. They smuggled in bottles of scotch and new jokes with which to spark their own private cocktail hour. It managed to take her mind off her problems since she could focus on wearing glamorous negligees to greet her guests. It was presumed the hospital staff closed their eyes to the situation because they did not want to start another ruckus with my mother, or perhaps because of the Clarks' generous contributions to the hospital.

Willis died November 3, 1964, as a result of complications from the carotid artery operation. A cerebral hemorrhage was listed as the official cause of his death. Maybe the advancements in medicine during the ensuing fifty plus years might have kept him alive longer—surely many have considered this having lost a loved one at a time when certain surgical procedures were in their infancy.

CHAPTER 22

"EBB TIDE"

When did Ethel's downturn begin? It's hard to peg a precise time. Maybe the accumulation of tragic, emotional, and stressful events triggered the start. In retrospect, there were lots of danger signals that heralded trouble. Trying to turn back the pages, I believe that Ethel and Willis both were beginning to experience certain physical problems that took them to the Hollywood Presbyterian Hospital for medical checkups in the 1950s. As could almost be expected, Ethel became enchanted with Dr. Stuart Knox, and so Ethel and Willis responded quite generously to his requests for funding for the hospital. What Dr. Knox may or may not have known is that in Ethel's mind, this resulted in a big obligation of Knox to her and, to a lesser degree, to Willis.

Among some of the things Knox encouraged, or at least it was presented that way, was the importance of a couple of shots of scotch each evening "to relax their heart muscles." More scotch? The three of them (Ethel, Willis, and Warren) already consumed a fifth of Ballantine's every evening while they played their rummy game. Anyway, Ethel happily obeyed Knox's instructions, with Warren following her lead, as usual. I noticed one time that Willis was adding something to his drink and found out it was quinine water. Quinine water and scotch? When I asked why, he confided it tasted so bad that he couldn't drink much of it. This was no doubt a way for him to be perceived by Ethel as doing his part in complying with Knox's orders while cutting down on his scotch intake. It was later discovered that he was having little ischemic strokes and dizzy spells, but he kept this a secret from the family. Drinking was a very high priority with Ethel, oftentimes the main factor in hiring some of the professionals. She liked a good time and that meant cocktail parties, and if a person couldn't or wouldn't drink, she wanted no part of him. Notice that I say "him." Ethel almost never considered a "her" as a candidate for employment.

Meanwhile there were all the pressures of the move to Monterey—building a new house in Pebble Beach, selling the old house in Hollywood, building a new facility for CTB in Monterey, and, of course, all the packing and unpacking, any of which alone would have been a severe stressor. In the meantime, Warren continually went back and forth from Hollywood to Pebble Beach, handling various details of the buildings and the move. Added to this mix was the pressure of trying to convince employees to move and helping with their moving arrangements. In two or three cases, Ethel made special arrangements as enticements, such as buying memberships in the local country club, helping with financing homes, and other favored assistance. In Willis's case, keeping track of the ongoing dual standardization with employees split in two locations was a real trial. He was also coping with some internal jealousies that had arisen over the proper treatment of the data. Added to that was the stress of the additional unexpected financing that was required.

One evening when some guests were at their Pebble Beach home, Ethel put "Ebb Tide" on the record player. During the rendition, she mentioned that the composer had met with her, that the setting of "Ebb Tide" along with the gulls and crashing waves were more or less her idea, and that the composer had used her ideas when composing the music. I guess none of us paid much attention to it because she often made exaggerations or bent the facts a bit to make a more colorful presentation. However, not too long after this, the same scenario was repeated, with Ethel elaborating even more about the arrangement she had with the composer. Still none of us ever mentioned it, even between ourselves. That should have been a red flag, but it was easier to ignore it than to pursue the problem further.

Her increasing sadness cast an ongoing shadow concerning the house into Ethel's life. She began believing the house was cursed after Willis's death some years later. She believed the very name Ebb Tide meant the ebbing of life. She tied the deaths of Warren in 1956 and Willis in 1964 to the name. Because her grandson Tim had given the house the name, Ethel held him responsible for the deaths and for her increasing unhappiness. It became a very real issue with her, and she began blaming Tim for the tragedies she associated with the house. At first she simply alluded to it, but then she made outright accusations. The atmosphere in the house with Tim cast as a doer of evil strained their once happy relationship to the point that Tim flatly refused to visit there. He was attending USC at the time, his schooling made possible by an education trust established by Ethel and Willis. Ironically his absence was even more of a sore point with her. She never hesitated to castigate me for my ungrateful son in almost every conversation between us.

At the time John Kennedy was President and was known to suffer from a bad back, he ordered a special rocking chair. Ethel also ordered one, indicating she was communicating with Mr. Kennedy. When Vice-President Richard Nixon visited some foreign land, she fantasized they had made plans for a secret rendezvous, so he could consult with her on grave international matters. It was incredible how convincing she could be. Sometimes it was almost impossible to doubt her no matter how far-fetched the subject might be.

Willis' death in 1964 became the saddest, most vexing, and most confusing time imaginable for Ethel. There was nothing I could do to help her. She had never properly recovered from Warren's death in 1956. Now she had lost Willis, her main support. She had never interested herself in the test development aspect of the business. With all the pressures from various factions pressing down on her, she seemed to make all the wrong moves. She turned to Denum, who all the professional personnel despised and thought was totally inadequate for the job. She sensed her hold on the company was slipping away, and her attempts to deal with the pressure with her usual indomitable self-confidence gave way to confusion and indecision. She became increasingly unstable. Sometimes while I was driving during our Sunday outings, she would try to honk the horn or even reach over and grab the steering wheel. It was all I could do to wrest it from her and keep control of the car. It was if she was harboring her own death wish.

I could not have prevented Ethel from drinking more and earlier in the day than ever before. Hers was a lifetime centered on alcohol at home and in the business world. Now she turned to that crutch more and more. She was not a happy drunk. After her second martini, she would become mean-spirited and belligerent even in public. She would rant and rave against smokers in bars and restaurants in an aggressive and obnoxious manner. Her disapproval of smoking stayed with her all her life.

I could not have prevented her, during her almost psychotic bouts of delusion, from calling employees, friends, or persons she barely knew at all times of the day and night and talking incessantly. If anyone tried to stop her or withdraw from her annoying behavior, she would turn on him or her with unbelievable hostility. It was discovered that she had a cache of an assortment of drugs she was taking to help her cope with her very strong mood swings. All of this, coupled with the alcohol, contributed to her outrageous behavior. The effect of dual addictions to alcohol and drugs varies in individuals. Yet each case of abuse shares a common thread. The alcohol and drugs alter the areas of the brain responsible for self-control, judgment, and emotional regulation.

Fortunately, years before, the Clarks had become acquainted with Ed Small, their next-door neighbor in Pebble Beach. Ed was a Vice-President of the Lincoln Life Insurance Company. He was a kindly, razor-sharp man who relished the opportunity to spice up his retirement with conversations about financial planning, the need for fiscal responsibility, and various top management problems. He had entered their life at the right time. Ed acquired enough knowledge about the troubles at CTB to give worthwhile advice. In fact, he played a major role in guiding Ethel through some of the hazardous days following Willis's death. He was great at analyses, and he worked with the Clarks on assessing their financial and personal needs. He was a rock for me too, offering solutions to help me cope with the effect of some of Ethel's outrageous demands on me as well as the CTB staff.

CHAPTER 23

EL CARMELO

In Monterey, a crazy circle began. Ethel would get incensed over some perceived slight and would take inappropriate action, often ordering the individual in question to do something that everyone knew was wrong. That person would call me for guidance. Ethel would not want to admit she was wrong, so she would turn to Ed Small, our neighbor, for reassurance. Ed would then call me to tell me about Ethel's "confession," suggesting ways to correct the wrong. He began coming to the office, and, although there was never any designation of title or responsibility, employees began to recognize his importance in keeping the company afloat. Ed worked with the auditor, Paul Lee, and with a local attorney, Allan Murphy, to develop plans to secure the company and preserve Ethel's financial stability.

Paul Lee had handled Ethel and Willis's tax and personal financial matters for many years, and it was he who pursued the McGraw-Hill connection. The Clarks had maintained another long-term relationship with a tax attorney, Thomas E. O'Sullivan, and he and Paul often worked in tandem to advise the Clarks on various financial matters. Paul arranged with one of the officers from McGraw-Hill to visit Ethel and learn more about the company. Fortunately that person was Robert Slaughter, a very charming and persuasive man. Ethel took to him immediately.

There are times I wonder if I could have prevented the sale of the company—or if I should have tried. Yet I know deep down that there was simply too much uncertainty over CTB's future with Ethel at the helm. It is questionable whether CTB could have survived much longer, and the welfare was at stake of so many employees who had devoted years of service and made outstanding contributions. The end was remarkably without drama. Escorted by Paul Lee, on September 1, 1965, Ethel apprehensively signed her name to the sales agreement, selling the company for $3 million dollars—the 2012 equivalent of approximately $22 million. Thus, she closed the door on her years as one of the most innovative woman executives of that era. Well, she almost closed the door.

Ethel received a flurry of letters from McGraw-Hill just before signing the sales agreement and shortly thereafter. The most important letter came from Edward Booher, then president of the book company division, who introduced Ethel, by letter, to Francis "Frank" Fox, who would be the General Manager. The letter was dated July 19, 1965. It described in great detail how Booher foresaw the company operating under the new regime. He elaborated on the many virtues of Frank Fox. As I read the letter years later, it was obvious that Booher's approach with Ethel was absolutely wrong.

"I have some good news to report," wrote Booher, "namely that we have elected a General Manager for CTB. He is Francis Fox, formerly Executive Vice-President of Silver Burdett and publisher of college books for Time, Inc. Frank is an attractive, highly intelligent young man in his thirties . . . . Frank in turn will report to Robert W. Locke, who has just been made Senior Vice-President . . . . Mr. Locke is also in his thirties . . . . I know that both Mr. Locke and Mr. Fox will want to take advantage of your consultative position and will need to lean on you for information, especially on such items as SCOREZE [which was Ethel's invention]."

Get it? Two *young* men messing around with *her* invention, one on which she received *royalties*. Couple that with Ethel reading an announcement in the local paper that she had resigned as Chairman of the Board of California Test Bureau, that June Duran would remain as Administrative Vice-President, and that Maurice Wilson (who had been with the company from the beginning) would remain as Secretary-Treasurer. Maurice and I became instant traitors in Ethel's view. There was a smoldering cauldron of hatred developing within Ethel for the evil McGraw-Hill, her worthless daughter, and the treacherous Maurice Wilson. Booher's blunder was that he didn't know Ethel at all. Had he known her, he would have substituted "senior" or some other adjective for "young" to indicate experienced men were in charge and that would have whetted Ethel's interest. She never stopped believing in her innate ability to attract men.

The announcement about me was particularly hard for her to take because Ethel had planned to send me to beauty school after the sale of CTB, so I would be able to take care of her hair and nails. Naturally she didn't ask whether or not this was something I wanted to do. Now, in her mind, I was gone too.

So imagine her state of mind when adding up the death of Warren, Willis's death, the loss of CTB, her perceived loss of me and the loyal Maurice, the disruption of her personal plans, and her misgivings over McGraw-Hill's honesty. She felt betrayed by all those she had counted on, and so she proceeded to do what Ethel did best—she fought back.

Could I have prevented Ethel's desperate retaliation? Not considering her emotional and mental deterioration. Not when her enemies existed in her mind only. Her strategy centered on causing as much disruption to the operations of CTB/McGraw-Hill as possible. She began phoning different employees, asking in a friendly way what they were working on. Then she would try to sabotage their work by telling Frank Fox what they were doing wrong. It was a nuisance at first, but it grew to be a real annoyance. She took pleasure in calling me with some imagined emergency, and then would use the call as a way to pump me about what was going on in the company, especially about how business was being conducted. She would lapse into lengthy harangues about Frank Fox, complaining about his management style and devising ways to get even with him. Her disruptions became a major problem as the contacted employees reported her behavior to me, or to Frank. It got to point that Frank told me to find some way to control my mother or he would have to let me go. Frank thought it was ironic that if only Ethel had behaved herself and exhibited some friendliness towards McGraw-Hill, she would have been a welcome addition to their social events and even to some business meetings. She would have loved to be included but, under the circumstances, that was impossible. Finally I had no choice and some harsh words were exchanged between Ethel and me, prompting her to ease off somewhat.

It didn't last long. She began hanging around the outside of the CTB building, peering into windows, and sadly became an object of scorn and ridicule. One time she actually entered the office through the back door and began harassing employees. They called me and I was faced with having to usher her out. She became so enraged with me that any form of normal communication became impossible.

I persuaded Dr. Knox to come visit Ethel. He used his influence with her and with colleagues to get her into a special home-like facility in Los Angeles that addressed illnesses such as hers. She stayed there for some time. When she was released, a male nurse from the facility was hired to assist her at home. Yet, even with all his training, he became exasperated with trying to control her or cope with her schemes. Eventually a wonderful nurse from the Monterey Peninsula, Ruth McCloud, was hired. She had the temperament to deal with Ethel and the two of them hit it off, bringing a sense of détente and peace to the situation. Ruth went along with a seemingly unending series of Ethel's idiosyncrasies and delusions. Ruth never tried to argue with Ethel or challenge anything she said, which was the secret of getting along with her regardless how outrageous some of Ethel's behavior was.

I couldn't have prevented the worst news. No matter how extreme and trying the situation, none of us was prepared to learn my mother had cancer. The origin of it was traced back to the time she refused to have surgery for fibroid tumors and instead turned to a new technique of having the tumors atrophied by X-rays. Doctors said that a large percentage of women who opted for that course of treatment died of vaginal cancer. In my mother's case, she actually bled to death from the cancer. She kept up a brave front with make-up, hair-dos, and beautiful robes until the very end.

It was only when she told me that a particularly lovely, diaphanous evening gown was what she wanted to be dressed in at her funeral that I, and those around her, knew she was aware of her impending death.

Ethel Clark died on October 19, 1969. It was her wish to be buried in a beautiful gown with full make-up and her hair done perfectly. She was laid to rest next to Willis and near Warren, in the picturesque El Carmelo Cemetery in Pacific Grove, California.

* * *

It was a lovely day in 2008 when I left the CTB/McGraw-Hill building, so strategically positioned to overlook the entire Monterey Peninsula. I paused for a while to reflect on my mother and all she accomplished in her lifetime. She conducted her first venture into business from her modest home. She turned a twenty-five cent investment into a thriving, multimillion dollar educational enterprise serving more than 18 million students in all 50 states and 49 countries. Ethel had seen and done it all. She had persisted through turbulent business encounters, endured personal tragedy and hardship, and fulfilled her original goal from her high school days to rise to a position of power and influence to truly "be somebody."

EPILOGUE

The transition of CTB from a small company to a division of McGraw-Hill, a Fortune 500 corporate giant, was in many ways easier than I would have thought. There was a common thread: both companies had active members of their families involved in management (well, one active member representing CTB), both companies were nonunion, and both had publishing as their objective, respect for their employees, and a positive interest in education.

I simply could not believe my good fortune when hired by McGraw-Hill. I was emancipated, and through all these years there have never been enough words to thank those in charge for taking a chance on me. I thought perhaps I ruined that chance in a pre-employment meeting with what turned out to be the executive committee of the book company. I kept hearing the members say "NOP" this and "NOP" that. At the close of the meeting Ed Booher, President of the book company, asked if I had any questions. I said, "You folks keep using the term NOP. In our company that term means Not Our Publication but obviously it means something else here." Mr. Booher looked at me in astonishment and replied, "My dear, in our company NOP means Net Operating Profit, a term I suggest you never forget." And I never did.

I was interviewed intensively about various activities at CTB, primarily customer contacts and operations involving inventory, ordering and shipping, and legal problems with licensing. I was asked to prepare position papers on the company as a whole, the strong and weak points. Somehow, the fact that our consultants were not under some sort of commission was beyond their belief and was one of the first issues examined. Things probably would have gone fairly smoothly if one of the consultants had not been about two hours late for an interview with Frank Fox, our first General Manager. Frank was steaming when Bob strolled in and, unbelievably, when asked where he had been, he answered, "Well, out on the golf course. I wanted to finish my game!" Bingo! This was just what they suspected all the consultants were doing, and this one remark turned our once cohesive and greatly respected consultant team into a group of suspected ne'er-do-wells. The result was an excise of a number of consultants, the installation of commissions, and a big loss of morale among those consultants who remained. Eventually the branches were closed down, scoring and reporting were centralized in Monterey, and the warehousing and shipping of test materials were handled from St. Louis.

One of our weak points had been a shortage of professional staff in the test development and research department. McGraw-Hill was willing to take that on, and one by one the staff was expanded with highly qualified personnel. All departments were put on strict budgets, and, as I suppose with all companies, competition developed between the various departments over who was going to get the money; and yes, indeed, there was a strong relationship with NOP. Personnel from corporate headquarters who came out at budget time continually reinforced that concept. When the purchase of CTB occurred, there was a rumor that the real estate department of McGraw-Hill recommended the purchase because of the anticipated value of the land. That, plus requiring the forfeiture of all of Willis's royalties before the purchase would be consummated, gave a pretty sound basis from which to plan the growth of the "division" that we were now called. Incidentally Tiegs, as a major author, absolutely refused to give up his royalty rights, and I understand the sale almost did not go through because of his adamant resistance, which turned out to be very smart of him.

The division kept growing and a new building was erected right across the street from the first one on Garden Road in Monterey. Harold McGraw, Jr., himself came to the groundbreaking ceremony. He and I had a nice talk one time about the trials of being a family member and the ever-hovering challenges of nepotism. No matter how hard you try, there are always people willing to accuse you of favoritism and ineptness. I thought he was a very thoughtful and considerate man and felt glad he had a son who would be joining the business and carrying on the McGraw traditions.

Having the sale of the family business behind me, I definitely could sink or swim on my own merits. One thing I felt particularly honored about was that shortly after the sale, I was named signatory for our division on various contracts and financial matters. For that purpose I had to be a company official, so I was named Assistant Vice-President, a title I held all through the 21 years I remained with CTB/McGraw-Hill, serving under five different general managers. Another high point of many was that the American Association of Publishers established a new Test Committee to deal with testing's unique problems with licensing, piracy, and legislation, both federal and state, and I was appointed Chair.

In retrospect, Frank Fox, the first General Manager after the McGraw-Hill takeover, was largely responsible for setting the pace and style of the new division. He also was new to McGraw-Hill, having come straight from being Executive Vice-President at Silver Burdett. He made us feel like a team, all learning about McGraw-Hill together. Some things really were strange. His first corporate meeting was held at Novato, one of the divisions in Northern California. About 12 of us were to attend with him, and, as there was absolutely no convenient way to get there (it was a four-hour drive from Monterey), he chartered a plane. He did not know it was against company policy to have more than two executives in a plane at one time, and he really got blasted for it. (What McGraw-Hill didn't know was that, at the same time, a number of the staff that were rock climbers were risking their lives roped together as they crossed the face of Half Dome in Yosemite National Park.) Frank's good humor, coupled with his earnest endeavors to make our division shine, endeared him to all of us, and he set the standard that contributed greatly to CTB/McGraw-Hill's future success. One example is the silver coin Frank had struck for all of us with the goal of $3 million in sales for 1966.

We were very fortunate in the various general managers we had, each coming with his special talents at a time when those talents seemed the most needed. The doubts that had been prevalent when we were first acquired soon faded away. Almost all these general managers moved to better positions in the corporate headquarters in New York City, and one of them, Dr. Joseph Dionne, who was a particularly far-sighted and dynamic individual, became CEO and President of McGraw-Hill.

As I write this in 2012, CTB has maintained its position as one of the most profitable divisions of McGraw-Hill over many years, no doubt with the impressive NOP that Mr. Booher was advocating. Just imagine what Ethel would say if she could see them now, that little gang of hers! I hope she would be happy, but she couldn't help but be truly proud that she had fulfilled her desire to "be somebody."

APPENDIX

The legacies of Ethel and Willis Clark and the California Test Bureau staff and their effect on testing and education are ongoing. The concepts they developed continue to be incorporated in new publications and applications. Profiling and highlighting the strengths and weaknesses of individual students, with the intent of helping the teacher help the child, is still very much a major purpose of CTB/McGraw-Hill. The company remains dedicated to assisting states and communities in determining the effect of their particular curricula through assessment techniques and professional consultation.

I have included an Appendix with some informative material for those desiring to know more about how tests come into being. This material also addresses how tests are processed as well as various testing movements in the United States. Two papers are included of the many research papers prepared by Willis Clark; the papers demonstrate his efforts to call attention to the importance of individual differences. I have also included a sample of a student's profile and a copy of Willis's *Diagnostic Analysis of Learning Difficulties*. For those interested in assessment terminology, I have referenced one of many online glossaries.

June Duran Stock
2012

Contents of the Appendix

Birth of a Test by Elizabeth Taleporos, Ph.D.

Standardized Test Development Outline by Willis W. Clark, Ed.D.

California Test Bureau: Test Scoring and Reporting (Late 1950s to Early 1960s) by Harvey Sullivan

Advertisement for International Business Machines at California Test Bureau circa 1938

Assessing Student Learning: Testing Movements in the United States by Karen J. Solomon, Ed.D.

Two research papers by Willis W. Clark, Ed.D.:

The Differentiation of Mental Abilities at Various Age Levels by Willis W. Clark (CTB, 1949)

Reading, Arithmetic, and Written Expression Skills in High School by Willis W. Clark (Reprinted from *Education,* May 1938)

Sample Student Profile

Diagnostic Analysis of Learning Difficulties

For those interested in technical terms about testing, see online assessment glossaries such as:
Assessment Glossary, CTB/McGraw-Hill, http://www.ctb.com/ctb.com/control/assessmentGlossaryTabAction?startLimit=A&endLimit=B&p=underAssess

Every test consists of appropriate items that assess the concepts to be tested. The goal is that each item is valid, meaning it accurately tests the concept, and reliable, meaning that subsequent testing using that item would give the same result. In her paper, *Birth of a Test*, Dr. Taleporos describes the proper development of items.

BIRTH OF A TEST
Elizabeth Taleporos, Ph.D.
Director of Assessment, America's Choice

The birth of a test begins with a plan called a test blueprint. The blueprint describes the number of each type of item that will be on the test. There are many different kinds of attributes that can be described in a test blueprint, but primarily, the blueprint shows the number of items that will be written to test each of the given curriculum objectives that the test will measure.

The blueprint might also show the number of items that will be multiple-choice, where students pick from one of several given potential answers. And it might show the number of items that will be open-ended, where students construct their own answers to a given question. The blueprint might show the number of questions that are at the simplest depth of knowledge, recall, or at more complex levels of cognitive demand, such as applying knowledge, synthesizing, or applying strategic reasoning to problem situations.

The test developer then engages subject matter experts to write items according to the test blueprint. There are a number of important characteristics that the item writer needs to keep in mind when writing the question itself and, if it is a multiple-choice format, the various options that students will select from. Common questions for an item writer to ask when creating the test question itself include:

- Is this something important about the area of concern being measured?
- Does the question address the objective of concern and not others?

- Is the question written simply, concisely, and clearly?
- Does the question make clear what the student is expected to look for in the answer choices?

Writing good option choices is not an easy task for most item writers. There must be only one right answer, but the other options must be plausible and their choice must reflect some basic underlying misconception or misunderstanding so that an analysis of wrong answer patterns can help the teacher as much as counting up the number of right answers. Item writers need to try and make options

- Similar in length, degree of technicality, level of discourse, and syntax so that no one answer stands out from the others
- Plausible yet clearly wrong because the student has some fundamental misunderstanding or ill-conceived approach to a topic or problem
- Independent of each other (if something is historical fiction, another option can't be fiction)

Good test questions should not carry baggage or demand knowledge outside of the content being measured. For example, an item writer who recently worked in a juvenile prison was unable to think of non-violent contexts for his items, and they had to be excluded from any test. The context would have potentially distracted students from the real point of the item, which was to determine whether the student knew the content or not.

Once a set of items is written to match a test blueprint, the items are reviewed, usually by a curriculum committee or representative group of teachers in the district or area sponsoring the test development efforts. The review focuses on the quality of items and the degree to which the item writers have been successful in matching the objective and other specifications of the test blueprint.

Items that survive this review are then tried out on a relatively small group of students to be sure that they are clear and that the option choices are selected by enough students to believe they are plausible.

145

Test publishers look at the percent of students choosing each option, and the correlation of the option with the total test score. If that correlation is positive and high, then high-scoring students picked the option, which is desired for the correct answer.

Then the items are assembled in test formats, sometimes as add-ons to live tests, such as state end-of-year assessments, where they are not counted in the actual test score but are used to gather relevant statistical information to decide whether they can be used on future tests. Sometimes the items are assembled in a full-test format that is given to large groups of students across the country that are considered to represent students at their grade levels. These students are carefully chosen to represent the demographics of students from all over the United States. They come from all types of backgrounds and include students with diverse ethnicities, socioeconomic status, language spoken at home, type of school attending, geographic area of the country they live in, etc. This information can be used to develop national norms for a test, against which the performance of future groups of students can be compared.

The test item thus goes through many different steps on its way to growing from its description on a test blueprint to its appearance on a high-stakes state assessment or a nationally normed standardized test from a publisher. At each step along the way, data are examined to confirm whether the item is working properly, and revisions are made as needed. The process can be fairly laborious, sometimes taking a few years from blueprint to actual live test, a truly long gestational period to obtain the well-honed versions that students take under high-stakes testing conditions.

Once a test is developed, it goes through a series of many reviews, including a psychometric evaluation by authorities on the subject and a projected cost of publication to decide whether the anticipated sales will offset the cost. Once the proposed test is accepted, it goes through a process such as the *Standardized Test Development Outline* established by Willis Clark for standardized (normed) tests. Most of the CTB tests authored by Dr. Clark were standardized.

STANDARDIZED TEST DEVELOPMENT OUTLINE
Willis W. Clark, Ed.D.
Director of Research and Technical Services, California Test Bureau

Phase I

A. Statement of test objectives.

To include the outcomes or subject matter that is to be measured by the test, the grades for which the test is planned, the grade range to be covered by each level, and the number of forms for each level.

B. Complete outline of test.

To include all the content that is to be included in the test. To include source material from which items are to be drawn.

C. Sub-tests.

To include a description of the content of each sub-test. To describe and include examples of the types of items to be included in each sub-test. Suggestion of the number of items to be used in each sub-test.

D. General outline of the Manual.

To include skeleton outline of the content of the Manual. This involves description of the test, suggested uses of the test, proposed treatment of test results, and suggested naming procedures. Some hint of general directions for test administration and scoring might be presented.

Phase II

A. Preparation of original items.

To consist of from 1 to 2 times the number of items needed for each sub-test of each form of the test. If multiple-choice items are used, care should be exercised to make all of the distractors plausible.

B. Examination of items for face validity.

1. To involve check of items against textbook or textbook series.

2. To involve examination of items by curriculum, research, or guidance experts to determine appropriateness of items in terms of outcomes being tested for and grade levels involved.

C. Arrangement of items in experimental form.

To include arrangement of items into proper sub-tests and the proper arrangement of sub-tests in the total test. Items can, by inspection, be arranged in the approximate order of difficulty. Wording of test items and directions for administration should be the same as is contemplated in the final form of test.

D. Key for scoring experimental tests.

To include the correct answer for each item in the test.

Phase III

A. Printing of experimental tests.

To insure format of tests and answer sheets being exactly the same as the final form of test.

B. Administration of experimental form of test.

To consist of administration of test to 100 pupils in each grade in the level tested and 100 pupils in each grade above and below limits of the level. Pupils tested should represent fairly normal and representative sampling of the types of pupil for whom the test is designed.

C. Scoring of test.

To assure scoring of tests and recording results in such form that outcome of each item for each pupil is available.

D. Item analysis.

1. To constitute a study whereby percent of difficulty of each item is ascertained. The proportion of the easy and difficult items that are retained will be determined by the proposed use of the test.

2. To constitute a study whereby the discriminating power of each item is ascertained. Items with greatest discriminatory power shall be retained. Some easy items of low positive discriminatory power may be retained if there are not enough easy items that are highly discriminatory.

E. Arrangement of test in final form.

To insure test items being arranged in order of difficulty for each sub-test with the easy items coming first and the difficult items listed last. If there is more than one form of the test, very real effort shall be made to match the items of each form in terms of difficulty, discriminating power and function. Since most of the standardization from this point shall be carried on with only one form, it is very necessary that all forms be equivalent.

Phase IV

A. Administration of test to standardization population.

To carry on the policy established by the California Test Bureau whereby a stratified representative sampling is obtained for the standardization population. This sample shall include a fair representation in terms of geographic location, sex, race, and intelligence. For this purpose, the United States has been divided into eight regions, namely:

1. New England states and New York; 2. The Middle Atlantic states; 3. The Southern states; 4. The Middle Western states; 5. Southwestern states; 6. North-Pacific and North-Mountain states; 7. South-Mountain states; and 8. California. New tests are standardized by securing an equal number of pupils' results from each of the eight areas. The results are then adjusted according to intelligence. It is recognized that as children go through school a natural selective process takes place whereby the general level of ability tends to rise. To take care of this situation, the selection of students for the normative population is made in such a manner that the median intelligence quotients for each grade are as follows:

Grades 1 through 8—100
Grade 9—101.5
Grade 10—103
Grade 11—104
Grade 12—105
College Freshmen—110

We attempt to set up a distribution whereby approximately 85 per cent of the population is Caucasian and the remaining 15 per cent is made up of Mexican, Negro and other minority groups. For most tests, a minimum of 500 students for each grade is desirable. If more can be obtained, that will be satisfactory.

B. Statistical treatment of standardization data.

To obtain the following types of data from the test scores of the standardization population:

1. Reliability—Determined by the Richardson or the Split-half method, corrected by the Spearman-Brown formula for all power tests. Test-retest method must be used for speeded tests.

2. Validity—Determined by correlation of test results with pertinent criteria, such as school marks, other test results, ratings, and other evidences of degree of success.

3. Norms—Obtained from the standardization population so that users can properly interpret test results. Where the data and uses justify it, grade placement norms shall be provided sub-scores and total scores. In other instances, sex, grade, and/ or occupational groups shall present percentile norms.

4. Inter-correlations—Obtained by determining correlation coefficients between the sub-tests. These relationships demonstrate the degree to which each sub-test is a discrete measure.

5. On occasions, additional statistical procedures such as factor analysis, regression equations, and differential norms may be deemed desirable. This must be mutually agreeable to both the authors and the California Test Bureau.

C. Preparation of profile forms.

To enable the test user to gain the most meaningful and graphic picture of the pupils' test scores.

D. Preparation of answer sheets and scoring keys.

E. Preparation of the Manual.

To insure a Manual that will enable the test user to make maximum use of the test, the general style utilized in the California Test Bureau tests shall be used.

As described in Willis Clark's "Standardized Test Development Outline," data processing was involved in many steps in the development process. Once the test was published, the users had the option of scoring the tests themselves or sending them to a processing facility such as those offered by CTB. Ethel Clark's insistence on the introduction of the test-scoring machine in the 1930s was the basis of what has become a major service of CTB/McGraw-Hill. Harvey Sullivan traces the development of scoring and reporting at CTB. IBM kindly allowed us to use photos of some of the equipment to further illustrate the changes made over the years.

CALIFORNIA TEST BUREAU:
TEST SCORING AND REPORTING
(Late 1950s to Early 1960s)
Harvey Sullivan
Former Data Processing Manager, CTB

Today, test responses can be captured in many fairly sophisticated electronic ways. Tests can be taken on computers via the Internet and on various machine-readable documents. Images of student responses can be captured with high-speed imaging scanners, and written student extended responses can be displayed on a workstation for a human evaluator to score. Tests can even be taken on hand-held devices and can be scored in real time via the Internet or can be uploaded to another computer. Artificial intelligence software can be used to score hand-written responses or computer-input test responses. Tests can even be taken using sophisticated voice-recognition devices.

Test Data Input Sources

In the early days of automated test scoring, data was punched into IBM cards regardless of the method of answering test questions. Student responses were very limited and usually consisted of true/false or multiple-choice questions with bubbles on a printed document. In the early days of test scoring at the California Test Bureau (CTB), these cards were either key punched or "mark sensed" and were then processed through various IBM tabulating machines as described later in the processing overview section.

At CTB there were three main input sources of student test data: Cal Cards, answer sheets, and SCOREZE answer sheets.

Cal Cards

Cal Cards were IBM cards with printed matter and bubbles printed on both sides. There was a single student biographical card where the student bubbled name and other information such as birth date and gender. This card was green so it could be easily differentiated from the other cards. There were test section cards that captured the student answers from test sections such as math, reading, and science. Each content area had one or two cards of responses. The student was given a non-scorable test booklet and had to mark the bubbles on the corresponding Cal Card. The test administrator was asked to collate the cards for each student: the student card was first, followed by the test section content area cards. After the students completed the tests, the Cal Cards were placed back in the card boxes and sent to CTB in Monterey for machine scoring.

IBM Cal Card
(Permission IBM Corporate Archives)

Answer Sheets

The answer sheets were a little more user friendly than the Cal Cards because test response information was marked onto a single sheet on which the student name was written. The responses were labeled with a letter and there was usually one correct answer and four or five "distractors" (incorrect answers). In the early days, these documents were not machine-readable and required a lot of manual work at CTB. Answer sheets were used along with a test booklet. The student would look at the item in the test booklet and respond on the answer sheet. After the tests were taken, the test administrator entered information (e.g., school name, test date, grade, and teacher name) onto a School Group List.

SCOREZE Answer Sheets

The SCOREZE answer sheet was a very clever invention by Ethel Clark to score test items "on the spot," allowing test results to be obtained immediately. The two-part document had a front sheet with a carbon back so the student responses could be captured on the second sheet. The document was printed so that the second sheet, which had the answer key, was attached to the front sheet. The student took the test from a test booklet and marked the answers on the two-part form. One advantage was that the test booklet could be reused and did not have to be purchased again when a different student took the test. When the test was completed, the forms were separated via a perforation, exposing the correct answers. The correct answers were those where the responses were inside the circles, and incorrect responses were outside the circles. To obtain a score for the test, you simply added up all the responses inside the circles, and that was the raw score.

SCOREZE answer sheets were revolutionary for their time. If customers wanted more sophisticated reporting, the front page of the answer sheets could be detached and sent to CTB for scoring.

CTB Test Scoring and Reporting Overview

Each year CTB produced a scoring catalog that described the various types of tests and options that were available during the testing period. The catalog provided guidance for ordering the appropriate level of the test for a given grade. It also provided a list of scoring reports and services that could be ordered when the tests were sent to CTB for processing. The catalog contained a scoring order form, which the customer could complete and return to order reports and services. The process began when the customer returned the scoring order form.

The scoring order form was used by CTB to fulfill the order. The materials the customer ordered were shipped from one of the four CTB warehouses. The customer order usually consisted of test materials (test books, answer sheets, and/or Cal Cards) and ancillary materials (test administration instructions, School Group Lists, return boxes, and/or envelopes). The School Group List was an important document for organizing and identifying materials when they were returned for processing. Customers coded school, classroom, and teacher information so the documents could be kept in the proper order during processing, and so the reports that were returned could be organized in a meaningful way.

After the test was taken in the classroom, the test administrator packaged the test and ancillary materials according to CTB instructions and returned them to the Monterey home office for processing.

When the documents arrived at CTB, they were sent to the receiving area, separated by document type, and placed on carts by school district. The School Group List was used to confirm that the documents were arranged properly and that the appropriate numbers of documents were present. The School Group Lists were then separated and sent to the keypunch area. The keypunch team would punch identifying information into specially marked header cards for use later in the processing. This information usually included district, school, and teacher names and other identifying information such as city and state. In addition, sequential numbers were assigned to schools and classes to keep them organized.

Cal Cards and answer sheets were placed in groupings called "batches," and then they were separated and sent to two different processing areas. A customer order might have consisted of several batches, where a batch consisted of a school district with many schools and classrooms within it. The headers with the identifying information were placed with the student test data. The processing of the Cal Cards and answer sheets is discussed separately.

<u>Cal Cards</u>

Cal Cards were delivered to the Tab department and processed using the IBM 519 test-scoring machine. The IBM 519 was a card reader/punch machine that was state of the art for the time. In addition to reading holes punched in IBM cards, CTB's machines had the mark-sense feature installed. IBM built these machines for scoring tests and many features were customized for CTB. One unique feature was the ability to read students "bubbles" from the Cal Card and punch numeric values into the same card for subsequent scoring. The machines had large wiring panels, and operators were able to wire them for each unique set of scoring rules. Another unique feature of CTB's machines was the ability to read only the darkest mark for a test item. The cards were organized in batches, with a district header card placed in front of all the cards, and school and class headers placed in the proper locations to identify the student test cards.

IBM 519
(Permission IBM Corporate Archives)

<u>Answer Sheets</u>

Answer sheets were delivered to the IBM 805 test-scoring machine for processing. This process was a lot slower than the process for Cal Cards. As part of the machine setup and prior to actual scoring, the machine operator would place a template with the correct answers into the machine for scoring the test. A correct answer template had all the correct answers marked or "bubbled" on an answer sheet, and a student document would be compared to the template to determine whether the responses were right or wrong. The IBM 805 had a large dial on the front panel with numbers from 1 to 150. Operators placed answer sheets into the machine, pressed a pedal, and the dial on the machine would move to the appropriate score value after it compared an answer sheet to the correct answer template. This was a raw score and represented the number of items that the student answered correctly. After the scores were recorded on top of the answer sheets, the sheets were bundled and sent to the keypunch area, where the student's name, birth date, and test scores were punched into an IBM card. These student cards were then placed with the header cards from the School Group Lists and were boxed up and sent to the Tab department for final scoring and reporting.

Some early IBM 805 literature stated, "An experienced operator can record scores at the rate of about 800 sheets per hour or call out scores to a recording clerk at about 1,000 sheets per hour." The IBM 1230 series scanners eventually replaced the IBM 805 in about 1963. These scanners allowed CTB to maintain the leading edge in scanning and scoring in the test scoring industry. Scanning technology has changed dramatically since these early days. Modern scanners can scan at a rate of over 10,000 sheets per hour and can capture bubbles as well as images of student written responses.

Scoring and Reporting

After the documents were processed, reports could be produced. All reporting was done in the Tab department using IBM machines that were designed primarily for accounting applications. CTB used the IBM 407 accounting machine to produce reports. The IBM 407 operator would wire electronic control panels to handle the various types of tests and reports that were to be produced. This wiring was the forerunner of computer programming, as it provided the basic logic to the machine to handle the reading of input cards and the output printing of score reports.

IBM 407
(Permission IBM Corporate Archives)

159

The IBM 407 was designed primarily for accounting-type applications, and it was somewhat of a stretch for it to do some of the more complicated algorithms and table lookups required for test scoring and reporting. The IBM 407 required a separate deck of cards to be read in to produce each kind of report. This was very laborious and error prone because the card decks would wear out over time or become jammed in the card reader. In addition, the printer was integrated into the machine, so if the 407 or the printer malfunctioned, then the whole operation halted until repairs could be made.

CTB had a maintenance contract with IBM so the Tab department's equipment could run for sustained periods of time, especially during the heavy peak scoring periods in the fall. IBM Customer Engineers (CE's) performed maintenance of the machines. CE's would perform periodic preventative maintenance to replace parts on a schedule (similar to the service on your car), or the CE could be called on demand for a machine malfunction. All the CE's were well trained in mechanical and electronic functions and could usually get the machine back up and running in short order. In cases where there were larger problems, the CE could call experts, usually from the San Francisco Bay area. One unusual requirement was that the CE's wore white shirts, ties, and suits (very unlike your auto mechanic), and they would put on a lab coats to work on the machines. IBM was a very conservative company at that time and placed a high degree of importance on its image.

In the early days of test scoring and reporting, the score reports were very limited. CTB used the most up-to-date and modern printers for the time, but the reports produced were still limited by the available printing technology. The printer of the day used a chain-like mechanism to print letters and numbers on a page. These printers were called impact printers and used a printer ribbon somewhat like the old manual typewriter. Printing paper had pin feeds along the sides so the paper could advance to each line and eventually to a new page. Because of the slow printer speed it was impractical to produce multiple copies of reports, so most report forms were produced with carbon paper and multiple sheets to produce extra copies easily. In the early days of printing, the carbon sheets had to be removed by hand, which was a very labor-intensive process that required many hours to complete.

CTB's Scoring department removed the carbon paper and broke the reports into meaningful units. For example, the breakdown of the reports might be by class, school, and district. Each scoring clerk had a metal ruler that was used to break the perforations on the form at the desired spot.

Reports were created by CTB for the teacher, principal, and district-level personnel, as well as for parents and students. Most of the reports were on multiple-part preprinted forms, and the printed information was tabular with rows and columns. One of the more interesting and useful of the early reports was the Individual Record Card (IRC). The IRC was actually an IBM card in continuous-form format, and student's names and scores could be printed on the front of the card. The customer could then keypunch data into the card, and this data could be used in their own systems. Another form of output was called a research card, and student data was actually punched into an IBM card. This data could be merged with other data in the customer's system. For example, attendance data and student grades could be merged with test scores to provide a wide range of information for the customer. Another useful report was the Right Response Record, which showed a plus for a correct test item response, a minus for an incorrect response, and a zero for a test item that was omitted. This report provided diagnostic information for teachers, who could use it to determine where students needed help. Yet another useful report was the Cal Stick Labels, which were individual student labels printed on a continuous form that could be peeled off and placed on report cards or on permanent student records, which could follow the student from one location to another and even to another state.

IBM 1401
(Permission IBM Corporate Archives)

<u>CTB Installs the IBM 1401 Computer</u>

In 1961 the IBM 1401, the first real computer at CTB, replaced the IBM 407. This was a much-anticipated upgrade, and it completely revolutionized how CTB processed tests and provided scoring and reporting products. In addition, a more modern printer was attached to the 1401. This was the 1403 printer, and it was far more versatile and faster than the earlier printers. The 1403 printer was connected to the 1401 computer, but the printer did not take the whole system down if it malfunctioned. Another important addition was the IBM 729 magnetic tape unit. The original configuration contained four of these units. Magnetic tape essentially replaced many of the former card functions and created another method to supply data to customers.

The following is from an IBM press release distributed on October 5, 1959, shortly after the 1401 was announced:

The all-transistorized IBM 1401 Data Processing System places the features found in electronic data processing systems at the disposal of smaller businesses, previously limited to the use of conventional punched card equipment. These features include: high speed card punching and reading, magnetic tape input and output, high speed printing, stored program, and arithmetic and logical ability.

Speed: In one minute, the 1401 Processing Unit can perform 193,300 additions (eight-digit numbers) or 25,000 multiplications (six-digit numbers by four-digit numbers).

A very bright programmer, who had written a similar application, came to CTB from the nearby Naval Postgraduate School and implemented the "monitor" system. The monitor was somewhat like an early version of an operating system, whereby programs were stored on magnetic tape and called in as they were needed. In addition, a sort program was stored on the tape and called in to provide various sorts of customer data. Reports could easily be alphabetized or sorted on some other criteria such as high to low on a score value (e.g., total raw score).

Sorting could be accomplished on the Tab equipment but it was time consuming because the cards had to be sent through a card sorter device, and sorts were done on a character-by-character basis.

CTB Installs the IBM 1232 Scanner

In 1964 CTB installed two IBM 1232 scanners. These scanners were a vast improvement over the existing method as they eliminated the use of the smaller IBM card and allowed CTB to use a full-page 8-1/2 by 11 answer document. The 1232 scanner essentially made the IBM 519 mark-sense punch machine and the 805 test-scoring machine obsolete. The physical size of an IBM mark-sense card was a real problem when it was used for capturing test responses. Many cards were required in order to capture responses for one student test. The 1232 used a full sheet of paper for capturing responses, which greatly expanded the number of items that could be captured on one sheet of paper. This sheet of paper had identifying marks preprinted on it and had timing tracks down the side so the scanner could coordinate student responses from locations on the sheet. The document was called an answer sheet and was much like its predecessor that was used on the IBM 805. The major difference was the speed of capturing data. While the IBM 805 could capture about 800 sheets per hour, the 1232 could scan both sides of over 2000 sheets per hour.

In the early days, scanning documents at CTB was the primary bottleneck in the whole scoring and reporting system. It required that the scanners were operated on multiple shifts and seven days per week in order to meet capacity requirements.

IBM 1232
(Permission IBM Corporate Archives)

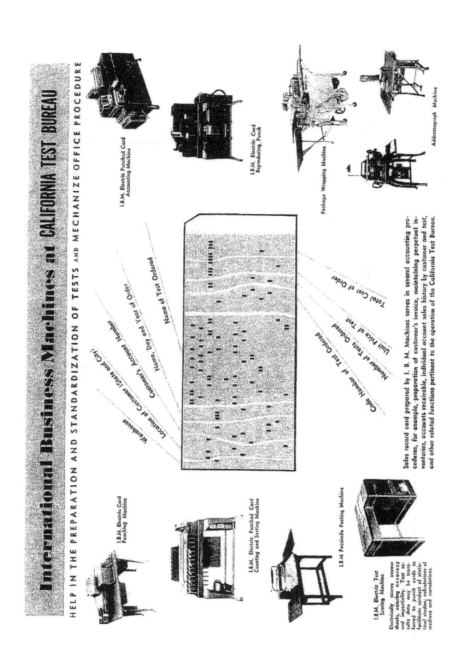

IBM Advertisement circa 1938
(Permission IBM Corporate Archives)

In this comprehensive paper, Dr. Solomon addresses attitudes toward testing throughout the years, including such varying concepts as "Progressive Education" and "No Child Left Behind." (Reprinted with the author's permission.)

ASSESSING STUDENT LEARNING: TESTING MOVEMENTS IN THE UNITED STATES

Karen J. Solomon, Ed.D.
Vice President for Accreditation Relations
Higher Learning Commission of the North Central Association of Colleges and Schools

Since the early years, the oversight of education in the United States has been highly localized. Oversight was originally based in the communities but was eventually moved under the control of the states. The growth of student populations has been steadily rising over the years. Within 80 years, the proportion of 14- to 17-year-olds in high school grew to 94% in 1970 from 7% in 1890 (Kaestle, 2000). In order for students to be reviewed on an aggregate basis, testing has evolved over time. Progressive education, one of many models, continues to have a role in the classroom, and its basic premises were built within Willis Clark's testing efforts.

Progressive Education

The Progressive Education Movement began in the context of expanding educational expectations. The education system was built on the idea of creating efficiencies in the educational structure—that is, identifying and recognizing those people with the expertise to create a strong curriculum and professionalizing teachers and administrators. The reformers moved to centralize schools. Although John Dewey is often cited as the founder of progressive education, several other educators, including William Kilpatrick, Ellsworth Collings, Francis Parker, Harold Rugg, and Ella Flagg Young, are also identified as leaders of the movement (Norris, 2004; Hayes, 2006). Some of these leaders were researchers; others were involved in leading large education systems, often in urban settings.

The Progressive Movement took place primarily from the 1880s to the early 1940s as the United States became more urban focused, and various social services and organizations began to focus on educational improvement instead of expansion. The progressives looked to expand the function of the school to include concern for health, vocation, and quality of family and community life. In doing so, progressives expected instruction to be tailored to the different populations of students who were entering the education systems (Cremin, 1988). Common components of progressive education included (a) a focus on the needs of the child, including the child's physical and emotional growth and total development; (b) generic problem-solving skills instead of a body of common content; (c) practical applications through natural situations; and (d) the acceptance that all students could succeed in their own way (Norris, 2004). Although supposedly modern, the focus on natural curiosity, as identifed in Aristotle's *Metaphysics*, did not survive conventional education. Small classes, appropriate equipment, strong pedagogical preparation of teachers, ongoing support, and the flexibility to adjust curriculum accordingly were deemed the standard elements of progressive education (Hook, 1945).

While the educational environment was undergoing major changes, the country was also in the midst of increased labor activism, debates regarding women's rights, and implementation of child labor laws. It was a time of change in the country's history that was unprecented and continues to impact society in the 21st century. In the late 1890s, Joseph M. Rice (Cremin, 1988) studied the differences in public education systems and wrote on the variances between rote learning and the active, engaged, vibrant environments that could be found across economic levels and across the country. He later wrote on the concept of the "progressive school" where students could learn in an engaged setting, separated from politics yet framed within a scientific environment. The New York-based doctor was critical of the political influence and underprepared faculty (and administration) in the public schools. This writing called for nationwide school reform. Under his model, teachers would be encouraged to continually improve performance. At the time of the country's progressive expansion and development, it seemed fitting that an education system would also be developed in order to meet society's needs. The progressive education movement called for child-centered pedagogy and equal treatment of all children regardless of race. The adoption of the movement sped across the country, and by 1919 the Progressive Education Association was founded (Cremin, 1988). Key factors of the concept called for a broader involvement of schools *within* the community, active and engaging pedagogy, customization of curriculum for different groups of students, and improved management of schools. Other elements were added over time until the movement began to fade in the 1940s. As the population of students became increasingly more diverse, it was evident that scientifically based research would be needed to provide the necessary evidence of learning and to develop curricula to address a wider range of issues.

Some claim the shift in educational ideology was a political agenda, as various political, ethnic, religious, and class factions at the time were fighting the growing sophistication of other organized groups. The reformers proposed that education should have nothing to do with politics, should not be a political party issue, and should be insulated from the formal political process through such devices as nonpartisan elections and appointive boards (Kaestle, 2000; Jackson & Miller, 2009). Others viewed any form of social reform negatively and looked to improve the outcomes of students by pushing for a narrow curriculum of which students could demonstrate knowledge, though limited, in a short amount of time. Progressive educators viewed education as one of the foundations of democracy, but the idea of preparation for citizenship began to fade as education for economic purposes grew. A highly educated workforce became the concern of many involved in the economic and political sectors (McDonnell, 2000). The ideas of progressive education have continued to move in and out of the educational discussion, though the Progressive Education Association officially closed its doors in 1955 (Van Til, 1974).

Beginning in the early 1980s, and continuing for more than 10 years, Republican administrations ushered in expectations of standards and achievement, which, in retrospect, were the exact opposite of the intentions of the progressive movement. The terms *accountability* and *transparency* began to indicate success in meeting educational outcomes, and the government (and the public) increasingly expected schools to provide detailed information regarding student scores (Hayes, 2006). As transformative thinking has brought about some of the greatest ideas of the decade of the 1980s, such as the computer and the Internet, the call for support of engaging students' natural curiousity continues.

The tides have begun to shift once again as districts are not only increasingly relying on standardized tests but focusing on learner-centered learning activities in order to develop students with complex thinking skills and an understanding of the civic responsibilities they would encounter as adults. The current service-learning movement provides evidence that there is still a great deal of emphasis on learning by doing. In 2010 students are often expected to complete community service activities as a graduation requirement, not only to improve their chances for entrance into a competitive college or university, but also to help them bulid a lifelong pattern of involvement. The country's reliance on an engaged society that maintains the democratic structure calls for a citizenry with a wide range of understanding. An emerging focus on civic engagement is based on concerns of a population with a decreased engagement in their communities and the democratic processes at the local and national levels.

There is collective worry among many educators—and the public—that the focus on accountability has resulted in a decline of citizens with the critical-thinking abilities that are provided by a broad liberal education. The concern that students are not engaged in critical self-examination within the context of wide-ranging opinions may not be described as progressive education. The current focus on test scores might have broad-reaching impact in the future, as students have not been prepared for political participation and are not capable of civil disagreement. Though the No Child Left Behind Act (referred to as NCLB and pronounced "nickel bee") promotes the view that the purpose of an education is to prepare the next generation "to maintain and extend the economic success of the United States," progressive educators continue to push for the transformative and humanistic goals of education. Today's progressives consider the educational vision of the United States in the context of sustainability (socially and environmentally) beyond the generation of wealth and a standing in global rankings that has been the foundation for most of the educational reform launched in recent years (Shaker, 2008).

According to Roth (2010), the call for a pragmatic, reflexive approach to education might be needed, more than ever, to develop the next wave of citizen leaders to charter the course in an expanding global environment but, more importantly, to help students find what they love to do and to chart their own life course.

Early History of Education Systems

In the mid-1600s, the predominately European dual system of education was practiced: The upper classes received formal instruction while the lower classes engaged primarily in apprentice training (Van Til, 1974). An evolving focus on religious study began to shape an education system that was quite different from the European model. There was little separation of church and state, which often led to a strong emphasis on religious training. Some states began to require parents to be responsible for ensuring that their students were educated. Public funds were rarely available, so families often had to provide money to support the local schools. Often this caused the funding to be uneven and in some areas absent. In the mid-1780s, national legislation regarding the development of land was passed, which required each township to perserve a section for educational purposes. In the early years, the schools were run individually with a curriculum set forth by the local school board, the parents, or even the lead teacher. The United States Constitution contained no specific language regarding a national framework of education, and silence on this subject provided the foundation for each state to control the education of its citizens.

After the Civil War, families began to move away from farms to the cities to work in factories in order to survive and create a better life. Meanwhile, the immigrant population continued to expand. Many of these new residents also worked in the factories, instead of moving to the countryside as previous generations of immigrants had done. Education was the focus of many scholars when they wrote about the need for long-term societal reform. Schools developed rapidly, especially in the urban areas, and became more focused on career preparation in an effort to bring more equality to the social classes (Cremin, 1988).

By the mid-1800s, Horace Mann's vision of the creation of mass schooling systems in urban environments began to emerge just as the politics of education grew more complicated and embedded within rapidly growing systems (Cremin, 1988). Mann, and many others, called for a common school ideology. Children were expected to receive an education on morals and virtues, with the expectation that this form of education would, in large part, eliminate crime and corruption yet support a country of free people. This concept took shape within a system of public schools, which remains in place to this day. Mann also concluded that common schooling would redistribute the wealth of society by educating the masses, thus creating an improved labor force that would have the ability to move earned wages through the country's monetary system.

During this time of rapid expansion, there was a tendency to group schools into districts and to develop more robust administrative structures to oversee the curriculum and finances. Various political and religious factions spent a great deal of energy trying to control what curriculum was taught and who would be actually engaged in the teaching. Political patronage was ongoing, yet the centralization of curriculum and the advanced preparation of teachers diminished the direct involvement of political parties in school governance. Crime and corruption were also evident in the education systems (Spring, 1994). In large cities, governments saw school systems as part of the patronage system, and in various ways education became a business as school boards contracted for textbooks and other services. At the same time, educational administrations were becoming more professionalized, and systems of multiple layers of bureaucracy flourished (McDonnell, 2000). According to Clifford (1973), the United States had 150,000 local school districts in 1900 that were eventually unified and consolidated to only 15,000 by 1970.

Testing Emerges

Although testing was prevalent in Europe in the mid- to late 1800s, the education system in the United States was in its infancy. Most examinations were given orally, and testing gradually began to be used across the country. In 1845 the Boston school system attempted to use short-answer tests by sampling about 500 of the 7,000-student population in an effort to measure student learning in a uniform way. The test results indicated that students' writing showed many grammar, punctuation, and spelling errors. This information was a shock to the community. When students were tested again, their poor scores created a backlash against the tests. Within 5 years the system returned to non-standardized reviews, such as oral examinations (Hoff, 1999). In another case, Portland created a uniform curriculum and developed a test to determine whether students successfully learned accordingly. The superintendent published each student's score, resulting in a public firestorm. In following years scores were not published, and tests were changed to make it easier for a higher number of students to pass in an effort to ease the anxiety of residents about the school system (Hoff, 1999).

Some of the initial tests were developed as academic performance decreased in the light of a growing, diverse population. Intelligence and achievement tests were built as a way to measure the science of education (Cremin, 1988). Between 1905 and 1908, Alfred Binet and Theodore Simon, with a focus on intelligence testing, developed a series of scales to demonstrate that, regardless of the quality of teaching, some students lacked the ability to profit from classroom instruction. The scales were designed to measure each student's "mental age." The initial tests could identify talent and help to place students according to ability level (Clarke, Madaus, Horn, & Ramos, 2000; Cremin, 1988). The concept of testing in this format was recognized as adaptable to a wide range of measurements (intelligence, aptitude, and achievement), and the business of testing began to emerge. Beginning in 1904, Thorndike and colleagues created instruments to measure uniform scales by applying psychological principles to arithmetic, handwriting, and other subjects (Cremin, 1988; Hoff, 1999).

In 1916 Lewis Terman, an American psychologist, created the "intelligence quotient," or IQ, which could demonstrate the relationship between a person's mental age and chronological age. Additional research and development resulted in what is widely known as the Stanford-Binet scale, which could determine an individual student's innate intelligence in a paper and pencil format. The study of standardizing students by groups, and the consideration of human development principles, became a key component of evolving learning theories.

Although there were many individual tests available on the market, there were few that could measure groups of students in terms of differences or provide retesting opportunities to show continuity in the original findings. By 1918, more than 100 standardized tests were available to measure achievement (Cremin, 1988). Willis Clark's initial work focused on case histories by gathering basic data (age, nationality, intelligence, personality qualities, physical condition, and educational and environmental factors) and studying the data to find differences across groups of students. His work, which reported population differences based on a range of factors, was of interest to many other cities across the country in the mid-1920s and was an outgrowth of Terman's research. During the 1930s, Clark created the Progressive Achievement Test (later named the California Achievement Test due to shifting sentiment against the progressive education movement), the California Test of Mental Maturity (similar to the individual Stanford-Binet), and the California Test of Personality (designed to point out personality and personal adjustment problems). The initial tests were designed to create a form of case history by use of group tests to measure these students at different ages or to retest for continuity. These instruments were designed to help organize students, based on the case concept, into the most effective learning environments—incorporating a wide range of pedagogies to meet the abilities and needs of the diverse student populations in the school districts. Over time, a series of tests were developed that related to one another so that students could be measured over a broad span of time. The tests could also be used as individual assessment tools (California Test Bureau, 1961). By 1932, 75% of the 150 large-city schools were using group intelligence tests to track students into ability groups (Clarke et al., 2000).

The first 30 years of the 20th century opened up avenues for the development of many instruments, evaluation practices, and educational theories, which remain the foundation for measurement today. The diversity of tests and testing programs can be characterized on three dimensions: (a) test type, or the kind of instrument used to assess performance; (b) test content, or the skills and knowledge measured by a particular test; and (c) the purposes for testing and selecting specific instruments (Feuer, 1999). Over the years, a wide range of measurements has emerged, which are utilized for multiple purposes: ability/achievement, admissions, the armed forces, language proficiency, nursing, personnel, psychological/mental health, and professional certification. Most performance measures are used by business, the military, and higher education, and as formative assessment in the classroom, with few examples of large-scale use for educational performance due to an array of fiscal and logistical challenges (Baker, 2008). Scores may be calculated based on *norm-referenced tests*—a measure of the level of an individual's knowledge compared to other pre-defined groups (students, schools, districts, or states)—or through *criterion-referenced tests*—a measure relative to a criterion or standard of performance to demonstrate what the student should know. College entrance exams are norm-referenced and are used to compare students with others who have taken the test. Criterion-referenced tests are often used as high school graduation exams with defined passing rates. State achievement tests also measure pre-determined levels of achievement and are typically criterion-referenced.

Intervening Years

For several decades, the term *testing* was commonly used, and as the country moved into the 1990s, the terms *student achievement* and *assessment* became nouns often modified by adjectives, such as *authentic* or *alternative* (Clarke et al., 2000). Authentic assessments allow for students to demonstrate knowledge through a wide range of activities, including tasks or projects. Consideration is given to the ways in which the students demonstrate concepts and skills through the completion of assignments. Measurements are often structured through the use of rubrics.

At first tests were used to assign students to educational levels based on intelligence or ability, but they were soon used to evaluate the quality of schooling (Shepard, 2008). Following the end of World War II, there was growing alarm that schools were too "soft" and that not enough attention was paid to the basic subjects, such as English, math, and science. The push to keep the United States ahead of the Soviets in the arms race during the 1950s was a major driver of the changing curriculum. Legislation at the federal and state levels mandated standardized testing programs. Researchers in the mid-1960s called for evaluations to focus on results, not inputs or resources utilized (Clarke et al., 2000; Hayes, 2006). By this point in history, the progressive education movement lost its momentum as more science-based curriculum was adopted.

With the adoption of the 1964 Civil Rights Bill, the establishment of Head Start, and the passage of the 1965 Elementary and Secondary Education Act, broader federal commitments to provide equal educational opportunities for American schoolchildren were created. However, implementation was limited due to a war overseas and violence (related to activities focused on the civil rights movement and frustration about involvement in the war) across the country, which drew on the government's fiscal resources. In 1966 the Equality of Educational Opportunity (Coleman) Study was conducted in response to the Civil Rights Act and focused on educational achievement. The study found that student achievement was influenced by family background and other socioeconomic factors, more than the quality of the school, in determining that student's success. The report reignited decades-old concerns regarding test bias that affected minority and female students. The basis of many of the early testing instruments was focused on a young male population, and while the tests have gone through shifts and constant adaptation, critics continue to be concerned that the instruments were not designed adequately to measure various populations (Kohn, 2000). Others charge that schools push students into less challenging courses that may limit their ability to gain entrance into competitive colleges that use only student test scores (Hoff, 1999). Additional complaints about testing focus on the fact that first-generation students have limited English and lack familiarity with some of the cultural or historical examples utilized in the tests, poor test conditions, minimal advanced preparation allowed for the type of instrument, and many more issues. These concerns continue to be raised even now in the 21st century.

In 1969, as a major demographic shift took place, the National Assessment of Educational Progress (NAEP) began assessing educational attainment. Mandated by Congress, NAEP surveyed the educational accomplishments of students, monitored changes in their achievement, and provided a measure of student learning at critical points in their school experience. It was also intended to model innovative testing methods (Baker, 2008). For several years, NAEP results were summarized for the nation as a whole and for individual states if they had a sufficient number of participating schools and students (DeVito & Koenig, 2001). Comparative state-by-state data were available with the publication of "Wall Charts," which provided information on student characteristics and education resources, such as per pupil expenditure (Shepard, 2008). This information was used by critics and proponents alike when debating curriculum and funding issues for education across the country.

According to J. Baker (2006), development of objective tests occurred as population increases forced educators to consider how to evaluate differences in student performance in a less subjective way than essays or teacher-made tests did. Achievement testing became a readily accepted way of examining student academic performance to (a) determine if individual students and their academic needs were met; (b) determine if program goals and objectives were being met by each student or groups of students; (c) predict future academic success; and (d) provide information to assist in improving, supporting, and enriching student performance.

The *Nation at Risk* report, published by the National Commission on Excellence in Education (1983), pushed another wave of review and reform in the 1980s when emphasis increased on the basics of education. Curriculum standards were created for every major subject while "high-stakes" individual student testing was introduced. Accountability platforms were developed for teachers and schools, or both (Clarke et al., 2000; Hayes, 2006). The movement from district-wide to state testing programs shifted rapidly from the late 1960s to the early 1980s. States rushed to identify or create tests. NAEP began producing state scores as a way to publicly increase attention to states that were not meeting minimum standards. Testing companies produced many instruments. Researchers and subject matter experts created some, whereas others were developed with an emphasis toward the profitability margin. Many of the instruments were developed void of joint state efforts. States could identify instruments that were "closest" in measuring the desired outcome. The information gleaned from the scores was confusing to governmental officials and the public.

Current National Expectations

As the level of educational funding continued to increase, it became obvious that the impact was minimal as reading and math scores remained the same (or in many cases indicated a decrease; Kohn, 2000). Around the country, many people recognized that the local governments had failed to adequately prepare students. There was a call for a new way of funding public education. In 2001, during the Bush administration, a reform act based on educational standards, No Child Left Behind (NCLB), was legislated. It required high-quality academic assessments aligned with state academic outcomes so that groups (students, teachers, parents, and administrators) could measure progress against common expectations. The Act purported that quality education could be identified in easy-to-measure criterion-referenced standards (Heilman, 2008).

The standards and testing movement, conceived by NCLB, viewed the purpose of education as a way to transmit facts and skills that prepared the next generation, who would support the ongoing economic success of the United States (Heilman, 2008). According to NCLB, students in grades 3 through 8 (and a minimum of one time for high school students) were to be tested annually in reading and math using state-approved standardized tests. The Act called for schools, districts, and states to use these instruments to demonstrate Adequate Yearly Progress (AYP), a measurement of students' knowledge of the curriculum standards. The results were to be separated into different demographic categories, including economically disadvantaged students, major racial and ethnic groups, students with disabilities, and English language learners (Hayes, 2006). The results of each district were then published in an annual state "report card" along with stringent time lines for taking corrective action, as needed. Schools were given at least 2 years to make the appropriate changes. If schools did not demonstrate adequate progress, then students would have the opportunity to transfer to other schools, receive tutoring, or participate in after-school programs; however, these initiatives were unfunded by the government. Although NCLB was intended to increase accountability so that states could identify and resolve problems, it has often been viewed as a way to strategize for tests and blame teachers, schools, or districts for less than favorable results. There are reports across the country that test results are considered when reviewing teachers for continued employment, though many union contracts limit their use. The results may be utilized by families when attempting to identify good schools, yet the difficulty and breadth of information is complex. The scores are only one of a broad range of factors regarding student achievement and school quality (Koretz, 2008).

While progressive educators believe education should be student centered, with an emphasis on the development of inquiry, imagination, and artistic expression, the Act requires curriculum to be scientifically based instead of focused on the whole child (Hayes, 2006; Lowe, 2007; Jackson & Miller, 2009). As a consequence of the emphasis on improving skills in reading, writing, and math (along with the expense of testing), many schools have had to reconsider the kinds of elective courses to offer. According to multiple reports, the majority of schools have reduced classes in history, art, language, and music in order to have more time for test preparation. For many, the testing and reporting requirements of NCLB has raised concerns about the expected speed of student responses; a lack of demonstration of logic behind student answers; and the emphasis on memorization of facts, definitions, and equations instead of students showing a deep understanding of ideas. The vast scale of testing efforts limits the states to the type of instruments that can be used. Open-ended exercises provide a complex way of assessing knowledge, measure higher order skills, and afford a glimpse into the student's thinking processes, but these are difficult to use in large-scale environments. Some of the factors limiting broad use of these tests include efficiency, higher scoring costs, subjectivity and bias in scoring, lack of comparability, and minimal generalizability (Clarke et al., 2000; Koretz, 2008).

At present, NCLB relies on the threat of sanctions against schools and states to induce greater effort and improved achievement without regard to factors such as heredity, family structure, and social environment (Shepard, 2008). States, districts, and teachers are to utilize information to inform curricular changes, identify populations needing additional support, create teacher enhancement and support strategies, and, in an emerging ideology, consider effectiveness of individual teachers during the annual evaluation process. Additional controversy has been aimed at schools' ability to reclassify students in an effort to improve testing results. Since the Act went into effect in 2003, there have been reports of states lowering their standards in an effort to improve reported scores. The methodology created in the Act creates incentives against two groups of students—the gifted and talented and the low performing based on the expectations of adequate progress (Shepard, 2008). It is difficult to collectively measure nationally the educational effectiveness of NCLB because all states have created and tested individual standards. Governmental agencies at the federal and state level use the aggregated results to determine state funding and support long-range planning activities.

Business of Testing

By the mid-1910s, tests were being sold to meet the demands of an emerging interest in understanding the breadth of student learning. Ethel Clark initiated a testing company (now recognized as CTB/McGraw-Hill) in 1926 in response to the needs of school districts to measure large populations of students. In the late 1990s, it was estimated that Americans were taking as many as 600 million standardized tests annually (or more than two tests per year for every man, woman, and child in the United States; Sacks, 1999). In all, 15,000 school districts individually chose which tests to utilize (Feuer, 1999). The wide array of information distributed from the different tests makes it challenging to measure the variance of education across districts and state lines. In 1998 yearly data from *The Bowker Annual* indicated ongoing growth and expansion of the testing market, with test sales in 1955 at $7 million (adjusted to 1998 dollars) that grew to $263 million in 1997, an increase of more than 3,000%, according to the National Board on Educational Testing and Public Policy at Boston College (Clarke, Madaus, Horn, & Ramos, 2001).

In 2002 it was estimated that the testing market was valued between $400 million and $700 million before the launch of NCLB. There are a relatively small number of companies (including CTB) involved in testing in the elementary to high school market, with only seven major entities in the educational testing industry. Five of those companies were founded between 85 and 110 years ago. Actual figures of sales and number of tests utilized are difficult to track due to the wide array of agencies and organizations involved (Clarke et al., 2001). According to the National Center for Education Statistics (2010), the number of students engaged in schools continues to climb, with a total public and private elementary and secondary school enrollment reaching 54.4 million in fall 2002 and estimated at 55.8 million for 2010. Total enrollment is expected at 59.8 million by 2018 (Hoff, 1999). Whereas technology has focused on making testing more efficient and less costly, questions continue to be raised about the appropriateness of particular tests and whether they are being used for the purposes they were designed for. At present, there is no structure in place for the regulation and monitoring of appropriate test use to allow test publishers and test consumers (states, districts, and so on) to determine the educational benefits of use.

Closing

In many small, discrete venues, progressive education models are being utilized to provide practical hands-on learning environments. Over time, testing has evolved to measure individual student learning in an effort to develop a strong educational structure to meet individual needs and also to demonstrate the effectiveness of learning for broad groups of students. Testing not only informs the public and individuals about student achievement, but is an economic force and has become a large, complex industry. In many ways, Willis Clark's research focus, with the development and analysis of tests, and Ethel Clark's role in building a business focused on testing reflect the broad scope of resources that are dedicated to the nation's ongoing study of student achievement. Recent research indicates that the practice of progressive education continues to be actively utilized in classrooms at a wide range of grade levels. As the business of testing continues to grow to meet accountability demands, there is (again) an emphasis on progressive education to meet the needs of a diverse range of students in the U.S. education system.

References

Baker, E. (2008). Learning and assessment in an accountability context. In K. R. Ryan & L. A. Shepard (Eds.), *The Future of Test-Based Educational Accountability* (pp. 277-292). New York: Routledge.

Baker, J. (2006). *Achievement Testing in U.S. Elementary and Secondary Schools.* New York: P. Lang.

California Test Bureau. (1961, March). *The History and Philosophy of CTB, Ethel Clark and Willis Clark.* (Available from the CTB, Training and Orientation Program.)

Clarke, M., Madaus, G., Horn, C., & Ramos, M. (2000). Retrospective on educational testing and assessment in the 20th century. *Journal of Curriculum Studies, 32*(2), 159-181.

Clarke, M., Madaus, G., Horn, C., & Ramos, M. (2001). *The Marketplace for Educational Testing.* NBETPP Statements, Vol. 12, No. 3. Boston College, National Board on Educational Testing and Public Policy. Boston: Boston College.

Clifford, D. (1973). A history of the impact of research on teaching. In R. Tarvers, *Second Handbook of Research on Teaching* (pp. 1-46). Chicago: Rand McNally College Publishing.

Cremin, L. (1988). *American Education: The Metropolitan Experience 1876-1980.* New York: Harper & Row.

DeVito, P., & Koenig, J. (Eds.). (2001). *NAEP Reporting Practices: Investigating District-Level and Market-Basket Reporting.* Center for Education, Board on Testing and Assessment, National Research Council. Washington, DC: National Academy Press.

Feuer, M. H. (1999). *Uncommon Measures: Equivalence and Linkage Among Education Tests.* Washington, DC: National Academy Press.

Hayes, W. (2006). *The Progressive Education Movement. Is It Still a Factor in Today's Schools?* Lanham, MD: Rowman & Littlefield Education.

Heilman, P. (2008). *Reclaiming Education for Democracy: Thinking Beyond No Child Left Behind.* New York: Routledge.

Hoff, D. (1999, June 16). Lessons of a century. *Education Week, 18*(40), 20-29.

Hook, S. (1945, June 30). The case for progressive education. *Saturday Evening Post,* 28, 29, 39, 41.

Jackson, B., & Miller, T. P. (2009). The progressive education movement: A case study in coalition politics. In S. McKenzie Stevens & P. M. Malesh (Eds.), *Active Voices: Composing a Rhetoric for Social Movements* (pp. 93-113). Albany: State University of New York.

Kaestle, C. (2000). Toward a political economy of citizenship: Historical perspectives on the purposes of common schools. In L. M. McDonnell, P. M. Timpane, & R. Benjamin (Eds.), *Rediscovering the Democratic Purposes of Education* (pp. 47-72). Lawrence: University Press of Kansas.

Kohn, A. (2000). *The Case Against Standardized Testing.* Portsmouth, NH: Heinemann.

Koretz, D. (2008). *Measuring Up.* Cambridge, MA: Harvard University Press.

Lowe, R. (2007). *The Death of Progressive Education: How Teachers Lost Control of the Classroom.* New York: Routledge.

McDonnell, L. (2000). Defining democratic purposes. In L. M. McDonnell, P. M. Timpane, & R. Benjamin (Eds.), *Rediscovering the Democratic Purposes of Education* (pp. 1-18). Lawrence: University Press of Kansas.

National Center for Education Statistics. (2010). *Digest of Education Statistics, 2009*. Washington, DC: U.S. Department of Education.

National Commission on Excellence in Education. (1983). *A Nation at Risk: The Imperative for Educational Reform*. Washington, DC: National Commission on Excellence in Education.

Norris, N. D. (2004). *The Promise and Failure of Progressive Education*. Lanham, MD: Scarecrow Education.

Roth, M. (2010, July 16). Good and risky: The promise of a liberal education. *The Chronicle Review, LVI* (40), B13-14.

Sacks, P. (1999). *Standardized Minds: The High Price of America's Testing Culture and What We Can Do to Change It*. Cambridge, MA: Perseus Books.

Shaker, P. (2008). A renewed vision of good teaching and good schools. In P. Shaker & E. Heilman (Eds.), *Reclaiming Education: Thinking Beyond No Child Left Behind* (pp. 163-181). New York: Routledge.

Shepard, L. (2008). A brief history of accountability testing, 1965-2007. In K. R. Ryan & L. A. Shepard (Eds.), *The Future of Test-Based Educational Accountability* (pp. 25-46). New York: Routledge.

Spring, J. (1994). *The American School 1642-1993*. New York: McGraw-Hill.

Van Til, W. (1974). *Education: A Beginning*. Boston, MA: Houghton Mifflin.

In addition to his many tests, Dr. Clark wrote and delivered a number of research papers, all, in one way or another, substantiating his belief in the importance of identifying a student's strengths and weaknesses so that proper remedial attention could be given. Two papers on this theme are included. A typical caution appears in his paper *Reading, Arithmetic, and Written Expression Skills in High School*, "While in the quest of wider horizons and areas of experience to include in the curriculum, administrators and teachers must not forget that each pupil must do his own learning and that the use of objective methods for determining pupil capacity and mastery of the tools of learning are among the basic techniques required for intelligent direction and guidance of the learner."

THE DIFFERENTIATION OF MENTAL ABILITIES AT VARIOUS AGE LEVELS
By Willis W. Clark, Director of Research and
Technical Services, California Test Bureau

This report presents an analysis of data obtained by use of the five series or levels of the <u>California Test of Mental Maturity</u> Pre-primary to Advanced Series. It should provide some further evidence concerning the age levels at which specific mental abilities or factors become sufficiently discrete to be of consequence in relation to both educational theory and practice. There has been much discussion of this subject but relatively little data for the lower age groups.

In a recent article, which was also his presidential address before the American Psychological Association, Garrett \1/ concluded that mental abilities are not well differentiated at the elementary level, while at the high school and college levels abstract intelligence breaks down into a number of relatively independent factors. On the other hand the Thurstones' have prepared <u>Primary Mental Ability</u> tests for all school age groups and, likewise, Sullivan, Clark and Tiegs have devised the <u>California Test of Mental Maturity</u> for all age levels where it is feasible to administer tests to groups.

<u>Materials.</u> The analysis of test results reported in this paper for the various series of the <u>California Test of Mental Maturity</u> were obtained as follows:

184

Series	No. of Cases	Median C.A.	Median I.Q.
Pre-primary	572	6 yr. 4 mo.	103
Primary	725	9 yr. 3 mo.	100
Elementary	1048	12 yr. 7 mo.	100
Intermediate	288	14 yr. 3 mo.	100
Advanced	600	16 yr. 4 mo.	103

\1/ *Garrett, Henry E.: "A Developmental Theory of Intelligence" The American Psychologist, Sept. 1946, pp. 372-378.*

There are 12 separate mental ability tests in the Pre-primary and Primary Series and 13 tests in the Elementary, Intermediate and Advanced Series. The test data for all levels are organized into a profile similar to the Intermediate Series shown on the last page of this report.

The reliability coefficients for typical grades are as follows:

	Pre-P. Gr.1	Pri. Gr.2	Elem. Gr.6	Inter. Gr.8	Adv. Gr. 12
Total Mental Factors	.94	.93	.96	.94	.97
Language Factors	.90	.86	.94	.94	.94
Non-Language Factors	.93	.91	.93	.91	.92
Test A. Memory	.90	.83	.93	.91	.91
Test B. Spatial Relations	.83	.83	.90	.81	.91
Test C. Logical Reasoning	.82	.90	.89	.88	.90
Test D. Numerical Reasoning	.80	.83	.89	.92	.92
Test E. Vocabulary	.80	.74	.90	.87	.93

Aside from increasing difficulty of content, the separate tests of the various levels contain test items that require the use of similar mental processes in responding.

Method. This report summarizes the zero-order coefficients of correlation and factor analysis data for the five series of tests.

The zero-order correlations were obtained by the Pearson product-moment formula. They consist of 66 inter-correlations each for the Pre-primary and Primary Series and 78 each for the three higher levels. It is practically an axiom in test construction that the sub-tests

185

should have low inter-correlations in order that more elements, factors or aspects of the subject-area will be represented in the total score. An analysis of the zero-order correlations should show whether there is a significant difference among these measures at the various levels.

In order to treat these inter-correlations as linear measures, it is necessary that the various r's be squared. These data are presented in Table I.

The distributions show a wide range of variances for all the test levels. The means and medians show what appear to be a nominal difference among the various levels, particularly the Pre-primary, Primary, Intermediate, and Advanced Series. The differences between the means, when critical ratios are obtained, indicate that there are as many elements in the younger levels as in the older levels of the tests.

The data for the various levels were factor analyzed by the Thurstone Centroid Method. For purposes of this report, the number of factors required to account for the variance (rotated factor loadings squared) for each of the five levels is shown in Table II. This table presents the percent attributable to each of ten common factors, specific factors, and the error (or unreliability) of measurement.

TABLE I. DISTRIBUTION OF VARIANCES OF ZERO ORDER CORRELATIONS FOR THE VARIOUS TEST SERIES, AND ANALYSIS OF THE SIGNIFICANCE OF DIFFERENCES

	Pre-P.	Pri.	Elem.	Int.	Adv.
Variances					
0.300+			5	3	1
0.280-.299			-	-	-
0.260-.279			-	-	-
0.240-.259	1		4	-	-
0.220-.239	-		-	1	1
0.200-.219	1	1	1	-	1
0.180-.199	1	1	2	2	2
0.160-.179	3	3	6	1	2
0.140-.159	3	2	2	-	-
0.120-.139	2	5	7	2	5
0.100-.119	5	11	7	4	7
0.080-.099	7	6	12	13	6
0.060-.079	10	12	7	7	9
0.040-.059	12	12	7	16	19
0.020-.039	6	9	11	14	20
0.000-.019	15	4	7	15	5
Number	66	66	78	78	78
Median	.0600	.0733	.0917	.0525	.0537
Mean	.0704	.0809	.1127	.0690	.0709
Sigma	.0484	.0472	.0944	.0679	.0555
S.E. of Mean	.0060	.0058	.0108	.0077	.0063
Diff. between Means:					
Pre-primary		+.0105	+.0423	-.0014	+.0005
Primary			+.0318	-.0119	-.0100
Elementary				-.0437	-.0418
Intermediate					+.0019
S.E. of the Diff.:					
Pre-primary		.0083	.0123	.0098	.0087
Primary			.0137	.0096	.0086
Elementary				.0146	.0139
Intermediate					.0099
Diff.÷ S.E. of Diff.:					
Pre-primary		1.26	3.44	0.14	0.06
Primary			2.32	1.24	1.16
Elementary				3.00	3.00
Intermediate					0.20
Chances in 100:					
Pre-primary		89	100	56	52
Primary			99	89	87
Elementary				100	100
Intermediate					58

TABLE II. COMMON FACTOR VARIANCES, SPECIFIC FACTOR VARIANCES, AND ERROR VARIANCES, ALSO EXPRESSED AS PER CENT OF COMPLETE VARIANCES

A. Sum of Rotated Common Factor, Specific, and Error Variances.

	K1	K2	K3	K4	K5	K6	K7	K8	K9	K10	(h2)	S	E
Pre-Primary (12.000)	1.704	.939	.650	.550	.327	.317	.207	.193	.105	.067	4.999	3.912	3.089
Primary (11.998)	1.238	1.082	.545	.494	.474	.427	.368	.265	.099	.064	5.069	3.850	3.079
Elementary (12.998)	1.355	1.143	1.135	.792	.614	.557	.389	.253	.165	.144	6.547	2.689	3.762
Intermediate (12.986)	2.359	.777	.471	.433	.389	.385	.289	.151	.101	.079	5.430	2.881	4.675
Advanced (12.996)	1.583	.916	.681	.527	.371	.345	.279	.217	.194	.062	5.080	3.475	4.441

B. Per Cent of Complete Variances.

	K1	K2	K3	K4	K5	K6	K7	K8	K9	K10	(h2)	S	E
Pre-Primary	14.20	7.82	5.42	4.58	2.73	2.64	1.73	1.61	0.87	0.06	(41.66)	32.6	25.74
Primary	10.33	9.03	4.55	4.12	3.96	3.57	3.07	2.21	0.82	0.53	(42.19)	32.12	25.69
Elementary	10.44	8.79	8.73	6.10	4.72	4.28	2.99	1.94	1.27	1.11	(50.37)	28.94	20.69
Intermediate	18.17	5.98	3.63	3.34	2.99	2.97	2.22	1.16	0.78	0.61	(41.85)	35.98	22.17
Advanced	12.10	6.99	5.20	4.03	2.84	2.63	2.13	1.66	1.48	0.48	(39.54)	33.92	26.54

C. Cumulative Percent of Complete Variances.

	K1	K2	K3	K4	K5	K6	K7	K8	K9	K10	S	E
Pre-Primary	14.20	22.02	27.44	32.02	34.75	37.39	39.12	40.73	41.60	41.66	74.26	100
Primary	10.33	19.36	23.91	28.03	31.99	35.56	38.63	40.84	41.66	42.19	74.31	100
Elementary	10.44	19.23	27.96	34.06	38.78	43.06	46.05	47.99	49.26	50.37	79.31	100
Intermediate	18.17	24.15	27.78	31.12	34.11	37.08	39.30	40.46	41.24	41.85	77.83	100
Advanced	12.10	19.09	24.29	28.32	31.16	33.79	35.92	37.58	39.06	39.54	73.46	100

The distributions of common factor variances, shown in Table II, indicate that about the same number of factors are required to account for the correlation matrix at each of the age levels. The specific factors and error variances are sufficiently similar to afford further support to this conclusion.

The relative weights of the common and specific factor loadings are shown by Table III in the proportion that they are distributed in the five sections into which the California Test of Mental Maturity is organized.

TABLE III. COMMON AND SPECIFIC FACTOR LOADINGS, EXPRESSED AS PER CENT OF VARIANCE, APPEARING IN THE VARIOUS SERIES OF TESTS

	Pre-Primary	Primary	Elemen-tary	Inter-mediate	Advanced
Memory	18.79	16.94	17.39	17.17	17.87
Spatial Relationships	27.45	27.99	23.59	22.53	25.05
Logical Reasoning	30.39	32.80	27.71	25.82	23.16
Numerical Reasoning	14.15	14.42	22.33	25.35	24.81
Vocabulary	9.22	7.85	8.98	9.13	9.11

Summary and Conclusions

Analysis of California Test of Mental Maturity test data for the five series with median age groups ranging from 6 to 16 years have been reported by analysis of the zero-order correlation matrices and by interpretation of factor analysis data obtained from the Thurstone Centroid Method.

In general, the data indicate that about as many factors are required to account for the variance in mental abilities in the primary and elementary schools as in the high school grade levels.

The practical implications of these findings are that teachers in the lower as well as in the higher school grades should know the specific mental abilities of their pupils so that they can direct pupil learning in an efficient manner. Likewise, counselors should take these factors into account in vocational and educational guidance.

September 7, 1949

(Reprinted from "EDUCATION" for May, 1938)
READING, ARITHMETIC, AND WRITTEN EXPRESSION SKILLS IN HIGH SCHOOL
WILLIS W. CLARK
DIRECTOR OF ADMINISTRATIVE RESEARCH
LOS ANGELES COUNTY SCHOOLS

MUCH has been written regarding the changing philosophy and purposes underlying instructional activity on the high school level. Among the points emphasized is the need in caring for individual differences and the adaptation of curriculum to the needs and capacities of pupils.

However, it remains obviously true that many high school teachers consider that their primary purpose is instruction in subject fields, and one of the most common assumptions is that they may rely on the elementary schools having adequately taught the essential skills or tools of learning, prior to admission of pupils to high school. In the event that pupils have serious difficulty in these fundamentals, there is a strong inclination to blame previous teachers for the difficulty rather than to provide appropriate learning situations suited to pupil needs and educational purposes as found in the high school.

There are many features in the modern educational program which have eliminated whatever merit, if any, this point of view may have had during the past. Among these are the following factors:

1. A changed policy in the elementary schools, in which promotion is to a certain extent determined by chronological age, the assumption being that high schools provide the place where adolescents should receive instruction.

2. A recognition of the existence of individual differences in capacity for learning, with the corollary that variable standards of accomplishment and degree of mastery of skills should be provided.

3. A less strict adherence to textbook organization of subject matter in elementary schools and a greater emphasis on activities and units of work. Unless carefully organized, the informal program may not provide adequate instruction in certain processes which are assumed to have been taught prior to admission of pupils to high school.

The writer recognizes the merit of a program in which growth needs will be taken into account in the direction of the learning process. It is believed that high school teachers will need to revise their aims and teaching techniques in view of the significant changes which are occurring or are now recognized to exist in the high school student population.

It is the purpose of this report to provide some objective information as to the extent of the problem, by indicating variations in the degree of mastery of reading, arithmetic, and written expression skills which are found in typical high school populations. These facts are not unknown to research workers and school administrators, but they have not been effectively provided for in the instructional program of many high schools.

Table I presents a tabulation showing the variations in accomplishment found in two typical eleventh grades in Los Angeles County high schools.* The data indicate the variations in degree of mastery of reading skills as shown by a reading vocabulary and reading comprehension tests, arithmetic as measured by reasoning and fundamentals of arithmetic tests, and written expression as measured by a language test which included spelling and handwriting It is seen that the pupils vary from an accomplishment equal to that of the average sixth- grade pupil (6.0-6.9) to that of the average upper division college student (15.0+) in each of the skills tested, even though the median accomplishment does not deviate seriously from the eleventh grade norm.

The significant fact is that relatively few pupils have a mastery of these skills on an eleventh grade level. It is safe to conclude that, as far as these two classes are concerned, and with reference to reading, arithmetic, and written expression skills, there is practically no such thing as an "eleventh grade" pupil. Obviously these facts should have significance in the plan- ning of the instructional program. It is probable that intelligently directed instruction would increase the skill of some of the pupils, but there will remain a wide variation due to individual differences which call for differentiated purposes, methods and standards.

As similar results have been found in other high school grades in numerous school surveys, these data may be taken as representative of the typical situation.

TABLE I. COMPARISON OF TEST RESULTS IN TWO ELEVENTH-GRADE CLASSES

GRADE PLACEMENTS

TEST	- 5.9	6.0 6.9	7.0 7.9	8.0 8.9	9.0 9.9	10.0 10.9	11.0 11.9	12.0 12.9	13.0 13.9	14.0 14.9	15.0 15.9	16.0 +	No. Pupils	Avg. or Med.	Act. G.P.	Dev. from Norm
Reading Vocabulary																
(School A)	..	6	5	11	14	11	13	12	15	10	1	..	98	11.15	11.8	-.65
(School B)	3	4	2	9	14	20	20	30	32	22	4	..	160	12.27	11.7	+.57
Reading Comprehension																
(School A)	..	..	2	12	11	8	21	28	9	6	1	..	98	11.76	11.8	-.04
(School B)	1	0	3	7	14	19	23	34	25	33	1	..	160	12.38	11.7	+.68
Arithmetic Reasoning																
(School A)	..	10	17	10	14	9	1	6	13	9	8	1	98	9.86	11.8	-1.94
(School B)	4	9	18	17	18	8	2	7	23	25	19	10	160	12.57	11.7	+.87
Arithmetic Fundamentals																
(School A)	5	22	12	16	8	4	3	8	6	10	3	1	98	8.63	11.8	-3.17
(School B)	3	16	8	14	16	6	14	14	25	32	11	1	160	12.21	11.7	+.51
Language																
(School A)	..	1	7	13	23	13	8	7	14	6	4	2	98	10.38	11.8	-1.42
(School B)	1	2	9	30	19	25	18	20	15	19	2	..	160	10.76	11.7	-.94
Total for Test																
(School A)	..	..	7	15	21	15	10	11	7	10	2	..	98	10.40	11.8	-1.40
(School B)	..	3	5	15	22	15	26	25	25	20	4	..	160	11.77	11.7	+.07

Read this table as follows: 98 pupils in grade 11 of School A showed a range in Reading Vocabulary from grade 6 to grade 15. The median for this school was 11.15, or .65 of school year below norm. School B showed a similar range, with the median .57 of school year above norm.

* Tests used: Progressive Achievement Tests: Advanced Battery, California Test Bureau, 3636 Beverly Blvd., Los Angeles, California.

Table II illustrates the wide variation which is shown by class medians in twenty-three representative high school eleventh-grade classes, with a total student attendance of approximately four thousand. When it is remembered that the median represents the mid-pupil of a given class, the variations of four school years in reading, six school years in written expression skills, and seven school years in arithmetic, the range of median accomplishment is startling. It represents a situation which merits attention and constructive planning by high school administrators and teachers.

In any event, high schools may not assume that their pupils are homogeneous with reference to the basic skills or tools of learning. It is incumbent upon them to determine the degree of mastery of each pupil, and plan an instructional program which will permit him to develop or improve the skills with reference to variable capacities and developmental needs.

Those engaged in the selection of references and textbook assignments should give consideration to the reading difficulty of the material, so that there may be reasonable expectation of its comprehension by the pupil.

Likewise those teachers who are directing learning in the sciences will need to assure themselves that the students have the requisite knowledge of mathematical concepts and processes, even though such skills are normally thought to be at an elementary school level. Students should be provided with a constructive and functional opportunity to learn these essentials as an integral part of the high school curriculum.

Thus, it appears that high schools, as units in the public education program, will need to give increasing attention to the learning needs and difficulties of their students. While in the quest of wider horizons and areas of experience to include in the curriculum, administrators and teachers must not forget that each pupil must do his own learning and that the use of objective methods for determining pupil capacity and mastery of the tools of learning are among the basic techniques required for intelligent direction and guidance of the learner.

TABLE II. DEVIATION FROM NORM OF MEDIAN GRADE PLACEMENTS IN ELEVENTH GRADES IN 23 HIGH SCHOOLS

———

GRADE PLACEMENTS

```
                 —    —   —   —    —    —   —   —            +    +     +     +     +     +    Median
TEST           — 4.01 3.50 3.00 2.50 2.00 1.50 1.00 .50   0  .50  1.00  1.50  2.00  2.50  3.00  Total
                 4.01 3.51 3.01 2.51 2.01 1.51 1.01 .51 .01  0  .01   .51  1.01  1.51  2.01  2.51
```

TEST	−4.01	−3.51	−3.01	−2.51	−2.01	−1.51	−1.01	−.51	−.01	0	.01	.51	1.01	1.51	2.01	2.51	Median Total
Reading Vocabulary	..	..	..	..	1	2	1	3	3	..	6	4	2	..	1	..	23 +0.13
Reading Comprehension	..	..	..	..	1	4	1	5	5	..	2	3	1	..	1	..	23 −0.06
Arithmetic Fundamentals	3	5	3	..	3	3	1	..	1	..	..	3	..	1	..	..	23 −2.09
Arithmetic Reasoning	2	3	..	2	3	2	1	1	2	..	2	2	..	1	..	2	23 −1.89
Language	..	1	2	2	1	2	6	3	2	..	2	..	1	1	..	..	23 −1.30
Total for Test	..	1	..	1	3	3	4	5	..	..	3	..	2	1	..	..	23 −1.23

Read this table as follows: The median grade placement in Reading Vocabulary of 23 eleventh grade classes (including all pupils in each school) shows a variation of from 2 ½ years below norm to 2 ½ years above norm. Fifty per cent of the pupils have accomplished above or below the medians as shown.

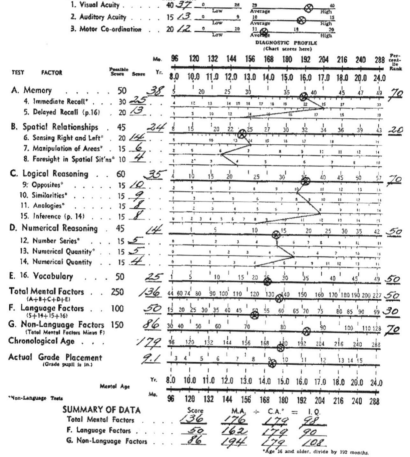

CALIFORNIA TEST OF MENTAL MATURITY
SAMPLE PROFILE OF A NINTH-GRADE PUPIL

TEST FACTOR	Possible Score	Score			
1. Visual Acuity	40	37	Low 28	Average 29	High 40
2. Auditory Acuity	15	13	Low 9	Average 10	High 15
3. Motor Co-ordination	20	12	Low 10	Average 11	High 20

DIAGNOSTIC PROFILE
(Chart scores here)

TEST FACTOR	Possible Score	Score
A. Memory	50	38
4. Immediate Recall*	30	25
5. Delayed Recall (p.16)	20	13
B. Spatial Relationships	45	24
6. Sensing Right and Left*	20	14
7. Manipulation of Areas*	15	6
8. Foresight in Spatial Sit'ns*	10	4
C. Logical Reasoning	60	35
9. Opposites*	15	10
10. Similarities*	15	9
11. Analogies*	15	8
15. Inference (p.14)	15	8
D. Numerical Reasoning	45	14
12. Number Series*	15	5
13. Numerical Quantity*	15	5
14. Numerical Quantity	15	4
E. 16. Vocabulary	50	25
Total Mental Factors (A+B+C+D+E)	250	136
F. Language Factors (5+14+15+16)	100	50
G. Non-Language Factors (Total Mental Factors Minus F)	150	86
Chronological Age		179
Actual Grade Placement (Grade pupil is in.)		9.1

*Non-Language Tests

SUMMARY OF DATA

	Score	M.A. ÷ C.A.* = I.Q.
Total Mental Factors	136	176 179 98
F. Language Factors	50	162 179 90
G. Non-Language Factors	86	194 179 108

*Age 16 and older, divide by 192 months.

Two individuals of the same age and identical total scores on an intelligence test frequently have significant differences in mental abilities. It is suggested that the following test data for another pupil of the same age, grade, and total test score be charted (in a different color) on the profile above to illustrate the situation. For further explanation, write for Bulletin No. 14, *The Proper Use of Intelligence Tests.*

Test 1, 35; Test 2, 12; Test 3, 19.
Factor A, 28; Test 4, 13; Test 5, 15.
Factor B, 34; Test 6, 18; Test 7, 9; Test 8, 7.
Factor C, 26; Test 9, 7; Test 10, 5; Test 11, 4; Test 15, 10.
Factor D, 13; Test 12, 4; Test 13, 3; Test 14, 6.
Factor E, Test 16, 35; Total Mental Factors, 136.

Language Factors, 66; Non-language Factors, 70.
Chronological Age, 179; Actual Grade, 9.1.
Total Mental Factors I.Q., 98; language I.Q., 106;
Non-Language I.Q., 87.
The corresponding percentiles are: A. 20, B 90, C. 40,
D. 50; E. 70; TMF. 50, F. 70, G. 30.

Diagnostic Analysis of Learning Difficulties

197